Inner Healing

Through

Healing of Memories
God's Gift —
Peace of Mind

Betty Tapscott

TAPSCOTT MINISTRIES
P.O. Box 19827
Houston, Texas 77224

Distributed by
HUNTER PUBLISHING COMPANY
201 McClellan
Kingwood, Texas 77339

AUTHOR UPDATE, September, 1981:

Since *Inner Healing* was first published in 1975, it has literally gone around the world. We have received thousands of letters from people who have been healed by God through the process of inner healing. The book has also been translated into German and Portugese.

OTHER TAPSCOTT BOOKS

Set Free
Fruit of the Spirit
Out of the Valley

Self-Image*
Forgiveness and Inner Healing*
Perdonar y Sanidad Interior*

Coauthored with Father Robert DeGrandis

First printing . . . December, 1975
Second printing . . . April, 1976
Third printing . . . June, 1976
Fourth printing . . . September, 1976
Fifth printing . . . May, 1977
Sixth printing . . . June, 1979
Seventh printing . . . July, 1980
Eighth printing . . . September, 1981
Ninth printing . . . October, 1982

Over 155,000 copies in print

Special, special thanks to . . .

Our children, Tammy, Paul and Steve, who on many occasions gave up time that was theirs so that we might minister to others. To them this book is dedicated.

Our parents who reared us in Christian homes, showered us with love and gave us a foundation from which we could share Christ's love with others.

And . . .

To all the people who allowed us to share their sorrows and joys with you.

But Most of All . . .

Thank You, Lord, for sending the people to us and allowing us to be Your channel of love.

Foreword

In a world torn with tension, strife and problems, the calm that Jesus brought to the storm two thousand years ago, flows over those who come in contact with Betty Tapscott and Inner Healing. In a day and time when the supernatural power of God is being poured out in great measure, He has graciously bestowed on this tiny little lady one of the most unique gifts available to believers. The love and understanding coming from the mind of Christ are apparent in her ministering to those who have been struggling for years for inner peace.

Somewhere in this book might be the answer to YOUR problem, whatever it is. You will thrill as you read of case after case of hopeless individuals who have been restored to normalcy through a simple prayer of Inner Healing. We can be born again, Spirit-filled, and still have scars left over from our earlier life which need inner healing. Jesus is the one who can walk right back with us through the years and heal those still open wounds.

As Betty says "Inner Healing is not just going into the past and digging up sordid details. It is not seeing how much garbage we can remember; it is throwing away all the garbage that is there." If there is an ache in your heart, or a scar from something that happened which you can't throw out of your mind, this book will bless you and minister an inner healing.

Betty and Ed Tapscott have tackled some of the most impossible situations (to the human mind) and have seen great results through Inner Healing. Read and reread this book and keep peace in your inner self.

Charles and Frances Hunter

Contents

Chapter I

God's Call

"Help! Someone quick! My roommate is threatening suicide."

The pine trees which only a moment before swayed gently in the summer breeze now seemed to reverberate the panic which suddenly thrust itself into the midst of our quiet little group.

"Please someone come." These pleading words drew our attention to a small figure emerging from the darkness. "My roommate is hysterical and is throwing things. She's threatening to kill herself. Someone help me."

Impending tragedy shattered the tranquil atmosphere of our prayer retreat. Only moments before we chatted pleasantly about the joy of being Christians. Now we were confronted with the agony of a person feeling separated from God. Panic choked off our words as each of us searched the other faces, hoping someone else would volunteer.

"You go." The halting words didn't appear to be directed toward anyone in particular, but seemed to be merely a plea for someone else to take action. "Why don't you go?" The question cut across our circle. "No, you go," echoed back. Suddenly all eyes were on me. The decision was made. Their assurances that this troubled soul would listen to me didn't lessen my feelings of inadequacy. I agreed to go on one condition, that they would get the camp counselors to come immediately.

As I started up the pathway, my thoughts tumbled over each other. Anxious questions intermingled with prayers. Awesome responsibility overwhelmed me. What could I say to a woman so filled with despair that she was threatening suicide? What should be done? Self-doubt almost suffocated me as one thought piled onto another. "I'm not qualified. I've never done

7

anything like this." In desperation I cried, "Lord! Please help me." He heard!

A beautiful peace welled up inside as I reached the doorway. I felt God's love and His protection completely surrounding me. After a soft knock on the door, I slowly pushed it open and asked if I could come in. These were my last words. From that moment on, God spoke through me, word after word.

Love and compassion for this woman flowed through me. She felt so utterly dejected, unloved, useless. A stroke had left her face drawn to one side. She had undergone shock treatments after a nervous breakdown. Her husband who was in the process of divorcing her was seeking custody of their only child. She had problems, problems, problems. One could understand her feeling, "What's the use? Life is not worth living."

I stood just inside the door for a moment then closed it behind me. Very gently I asked again, "May I sit down?" "Yes," she said, as she continued to pace back and forth. I walked across the room and sat down on the bed. The Lord immediately impressed on me to be still and listen. She began to pour out years of hurts and frustrations and feelings of rejections.

She would throw her hands up into the air in despair, clasp her head as if in agony and weep and say, "I just want to die, I want to die. No one cares if I live or die. No one cares." My heart ached for her. I assured her that I cared and loved her, that God cared and loved her. I emphasized how much her little boy loved her.

Each moment was agonizingly long and I wondered, "Where are the counselors, when will someone come to help?" I was still praying constantly. Suddenly, she quit pacing back and forth. I asked her to show me a picture of her little boy. She took a colored 5x7 picture from her suitcase. He was such a beautiful child. "Oh, he needs you so," I said, "What would he do if you killed yourself: How could he ever get over the hurt?" "He is the only one who loves me," she replied. Again, I told her I loved her, God loved her, and other people loved her and were praying for her—even at that very moment. She became more calm. I talked on as the Lord told me what to say.

Finally, there was a knock on the door. "Oh, thank you, Lord, the counselors have finally come," I thought. It was not the counselors, but my husband; he had become concerned about me and also came to relay the message that the counselors were not able to come. For a moment, I almost panicked. What else could I do for this lady? I must confess that there was a touch of resentment because the leaders were not coming to help. I felt that they were experienced and trained while I was not.

Looking back now, I understand what God was doing. That cry for help was more than anguished words. In reality it was a summons from God calling me into a ministry I barely knew existed—Inner Healing. The Lord knew I was the overly cautious (let's go very, very slowly) type of person. When I went swimming, I'd stick one little toe in the water then my ankle then hesitantly, my leg—all very, very slowly. But the Lord doesn't have time for us to do things according to our time table. That night, He literally **pushed** me into a ministry of inner healing.

Although friends had prayed with me for healing of the memories several months earlier, I knew practically nothing about inner healing. But through these experiences that night, the Lord carefully began teaching me how to minister in different areas: how to talk to a suicidal person, how to take authority over Satan and over the evil spirits he sends against people, and how to pray for Jesus to heal painful memories.

While I was thinking, "Lord, the counselors are not coming, **now** what do we do next?", the Lord said, "Bind the spirit of suicide." It was not an audible voice, but there was no mistaking that inner voice. We had never done that before, but again He said, "Bind the spirit of suicide." I asked the lady if we could pray with her. "Oh, please do," she urged. Then, like a precious, frightened child, she ran, hopped in bed, pulled the covers up to her chin and waited for us to pray for her.

My husband and I knelt by her bed. We asked the Lord to reveal the negative forces Satan had sent against her. As the Lord directed word for word, we had her to renounce in the name of Jesus the different spirits that were oppressing her. After we had prayed for her release from the spirits of suicide, depression, rejection, fear, despair, etc., she said, "But, oh, the memories. Oh, the memories." Quite plainly, God said, "Pray for those painful memories, and I'll heal them." So, under the leadership of the Holy Spirit, we asked Jesus to walk back into every second of her life, to heal every hurt, every disappointment, to take away every fear, to take away the agony of her mental breakdown, the trauma of the stroke, and the heartache of her broken marriage. We asked Him to fill her with His love, His joy, and His peace.

Praise the Lord! The peace of Jesus just fell on her and she was filled with His love. He calmed the storm that was raging on the inside of her that night. Just before she drifted off to sleep, I leaned over, kissed her goodnight, and we tiptoed out the door.

Thus began a ministry of intercessory prayer for inner healing. We did not seek a ministry. We merely offered ourselves to the Lord to be used as He wanted. The ministry that God ordained that night has involved my husband and me in countless hours of counseling and praying on the phone, in person, and in groups. Many are the hours we have listened as young people shared their hurts and their guilt feelings. There have been many more hours of listening as couples have shared their marital problems and resentments. Other times we have shared another's grief and sorrow. We have had many opportunities to show understanding and compassion as people poured out their hatred and bitterness toward mates or relatives. Under the leading of the Holy Spirit, many secrets have been revealed; deep, hidden feelings of rejection and loneliness, of guilt and shame, thoughts of murder or suicide.

Since that first night, we have shared inner healing many times in many different places with groups numbering from 25 to 1500. The Spirit of the Lord was so strong in this large group that for over an hour no one moved or made a sound. We have ministered by a beautiful lake, and to a group of dedicated Chinese Christians through the aid of an interpreter. The Lord has led a constant stream of people to our door.

During all these experiences, the one, the only thing we could do was to share **God's love and His peace.** Of ourselves, we could do nothing. God's part was to forgive and heal. Our part was to lift up in intercessory prayer, in faith, believing— and then, watch God's power transform lives before our eyes.

When a person is willing to forgive and to ask forgiveness and when a person is willing to allow Jesus to "Walk" back into his past, the person is usually set free and healed of his painful memories. Thank you, Jesus. He lives! All praise, honor, and glory goes to our Father, to Jesus Christ, and to the Holy Spirit.

Chapter II

What Is Inner Healing?

Inner healing is the healing of the inner man: the mind, the emotions, the painful memories, the dreams. It is the process through prayer whereby we are set free from feelings of resentment, rejection, self-pity, depression, guilt, fear, sorrow, hatred, inferiority, condemnation, or worthlessness, etc. Romans 12:2 (KJV) says, "And be not conformed to this world: but be ye transformed by the renewing of your mind . . ." Inner healing is the renewing of your mind.

Jesus said, "I am leaving you with a gift—peace of mind and heart! And the peace I give isn't fragile like the peace the world gives. So don't be troubled or afraid." John 14:27 (LB)* But so many people today do not have that inner peace. Many are Spirit-filled Christians, in good physical condition, but yet emotionally crippled. Jesus wants us to be completely whole. In Isaiah 53:5 the Bible foretells Jesus' role, ". . . he was wounded and bruised for our **sins.** He was chastised that we might have **peace;** he was lashed—and we were **healed!**" He wants to save us from our sins: 'Spiritual Healing'; He wants us to have peace: 'Inner Healing'; and He wants us to be free from pain and disease: 'Physical Healing'. He wants us to be made WHOLE!

Inner healing requires two steps:

(1) Breaking Satan's bondage and reclaiming our inheritance.

(2) Prayer for healing of memories.

I like to think of the first step of inner healing as "spiritual surgery" where Jesus cuts away all the "growths" that have

---

* All Scriptures are taken from the Tyndale Living Bible unless otherwise noted.

been growing inside of us—the growths of fear, hatred, anger, jealousy, self-pity, etc. Then through the prayer for healing of memories, Jesus walks back into our past and heals every hurt; He takes a spiritual eraser and wipes away every painful memory. He may not blot out the memory completely, but He removes the hurt and the sting. He anesthetizes the pain and deep wound. Then He anoints with the oil of the Holy Spirit and heals the places where the hurt has been. He cleanses us and gives us His peace. Colossians 2:11-15 describes so beautifully this spiritual surgery.

> "When you came to Christ he set you free from your evil desires, not by a bodily operation of circumcision but by a spiritual operation, the baptism of your souls. For in baptism you see how your old, evil nature died with him and was buried with him; and then you came up out of death with him into a new life because you trusted the Word of the mighty God who raised Christ from the dead. You were dead in sins, and your sinful desires were not yet cut away. Then he gave you a share in the very life of Christ, for he forgave all your sins, and blotted out the charges proved against you, the list of his commandments which you had not obeyed. He took this list of sins and destroyed it by nailing it to Christ's cross. In this way God took away Satan's power to accuse you of sin, and God openly displayed to the whole world Christ's triumph at the cross where your sins were all taken away."

Jesus is the only one who can heal our memories and our hurts, and through inner healing, He will if . . .

1. we want to be set free from Satan's bondage

2. we want our memories healed

3. we want to be made whole

4. we want to **stay** whole

"Jesus Christ is the same yesterday, today, and forever." (Hebrews 13:8). Time and space mean nothing to Him. He can walk back into our past and heal where we hurt. He wants us to give our past to Him. Philippians 3:13 tells us to forget the past and look forward to what lies ahead.

Some people enjoy living in the past, reliving and going over past hurts, and being a martyr; Jesus will not help these people. But if we **want** to be made whole, if we really want that inner peace, He is able and faithful to give it to us. Colossians 1:13-14 says, "For he has rescued us out of the darkness and gloom of Satan's kingdom and brought us into the kingdom of his dear Son, who bought our freedom with his blood and forgave us all our sins."

Inner healing is not just going into the past and digging up sordid details. It is not seeing how much garbage we can remember; it is throwing away all the garbage that is there. It's having Jesus shine His divine light in all those dark places where Satan has hidden those hurts and painful memories. It's having Jesus walk hand-in-hand through every second of our lives, of being right there with us during those unpleasant situations.

Often, we think 'out of sight, out of mind' *does not work* concerning unpleasant memories. But this thinking is similar to the practice of piling articles into a closet. When the door is closed we don't see the clutter, but eventually if we keep cramming things into the closet all the items will come tumbling out. The same principle applies to our mind. We may push "junk" (fears, resentment, guilt) back into our mind and think it will not bother us, but it is way down in our subconscious and most definitely will affect our emotions and influence the way we act or react. Repressed anger, resentment or fear will come forth at a time when we least expect it.

How many of us go through life fighting the battle of "If only . . ." or "What if . . .?" Someone has said, we should take two words out of our vocabulary—"Never" and "Always." "I **never** do anything right." "I **always** fail." "You **never** do thus and so." "You **always** do thus and so." The Bible promises freedom from these negative traits.

Fearful and frustrated people are consuming enormous amounts of liquor, tranquilizers, and sleeping pills trying to blot out past and present hurts. Millions of dollars are spent going to doctors, psychologists and psychiatrists. I want to say here I praise the Lord for Christian doctors and nurses. Luke was a physician and was inspired by the Holy Spirit to write the story of Jesus. God created medicines and gave man the intelligence and skill to use them, but divine healing is our Lord's highest. Doctors treat, Jesus heals. So often medical science treats our symptoms; but Jesus wants to heal the cause.

Christian psychiatrists and physicians rely on the Lord and we praise God for them. Inner healing is psychotherapy, plus God.

Jesus is the greatest physician—the greatest psychiatrist. He alone can make us completely whole. He wants to heal our broken hearts. Where there has been mental confusion, He wants to give us serenity. Where there has been fear, He is eager to give us courage and a sound mind—free from fear. Jesus wants to mend broken relationships, He wants to rebuild crumbling marriages. He wants us to be able to relate to others effectively and in a positive way. He wants us to be able to love others as we would like to be loved and to forgive others as we should. He wants us to be the person He **created** us to be.

If we were to use one word describing the results of inner healing it would be—PEACE. Think of some of the Biblical characters who obviously had a deep need and were given that inner peace. When we think of Saul of Tarsus and all the Christians he killed before he became a Christian, we can imagine the guilt and remorse that he must have felt. But the Lord forgave him, filled him with inner peace, and he became a spiritual giant—a great apostle.

Consider the woman who had committed adultery. Undoubtedly, she felt condemnation and shame, but Jesus said, ". . . Neither do I condemn thee: go, and sin no more." (John 8:11 KJV) David not only committed adultry, but he had Bathsheba's husband killed. His illegitimate, infant son died. Surely, he was overcome with painful memories. Nevertheless, the Lord gave him inner healing and David became a man after God's own heart. He wrote in Psalms 16:9 that his "Heart, body, and soul are filled with joy." Since **soul** means **mind,** this means he had a joyous mind—he had peace of mind.

Peter felt shame for denying Christ, but he received forgiveness and peace and became so well adjusted Jesus called him the rock.

The Lord wants to give us this same **peace** through inner healing. The Bible promises us in Philippians 4:7 ". . . His peace will keep your thoughts and your hearts quiet and at rest as you trust in Christ Jesus."

In Isaiah 26:3 we read, "He will keep in perfect peace all

those who trust in him, whose thoughts turn often to the Lord!"

Ephesians 2:14 says, "For Christ himself is our way of peace . . ."

THANK YOU LORD JESUS FOR YOUR PEACE.

THANK YOU JESUS FOR INNER HEALING.

Chapter III

Why Everyone Needs Inner Healing

I suspect Satan keeps a card file on all our "weak" spots, our "sore" spots, our failures, our embarrassments, our fears, our feelings of rejection and guilt. Satan is the one who enables us to remember word for word some argument we have had. Satan is the one that keeps reminding us that we cannot forgive someone for hurting us. Satan is a liar! The Bible says in Matthew 6:14-15, "Your heavenly Father will forgive you if you forgive those who sin against you; but if you refuse to forgive them, he will not forgive you." Complete inner healing can come **only** after we forgive those who have hurt us. Complete inner healing can come **only** after we give our past hurts and fears totally over to the Lord.

Every experience we have ever had has molded our personality and makes us act the way we do. We relate to others out of our past experiences. Psychologists tell us that what happens to us in the first few years of our life forms the basis for the way we act or react to situations for the rest of our life.

In Matthew 12:35-36 (Phillips), we read, "A good man gives out good—from the goodness stored in his heart; a bad man gives out evil—from his store of evil." Psychologists have estimated we spend fifty percent of our mental and emotional energy repressing painful memories.

Some May Need Inner Healing for **Minor** Hurts or Fears—

All of us need inner healing to some degree or another. For some, it may be for a minor thing. Haven't we all said, "Oh! I wish I hadn't done that" or "Oh! I wish I hadn't said that?" Of course, we cannot change the situation, but Jesus can take away the embarrassment we feel when we think about the incident.

We all have had times when we felt we were not understood: a friend may have betrayed us, we may have felt a mate let us down, perhaps way back in our childhood, a teacher criticized us unduly—really all minor incidents, but yet incidents that left "sore" spots or painful memories.

We may need inner healing for a fear that has been with us since childhood. There are so many adults with fears of water, dogs, cats, heights, elevators, etc. As adults, we try to overcome these fears, we feel embarrassed because of our "hang-ups"; we try to use our intellect and reason the fears away, but they become like heavy chains weighing us down. Jesus is the only one who can break those chains. God's Word says, ". . . where the Spirit of the Lord is, there is liberty." (II Corinthians 3:17 KJV)

The Holy Spirit revealed a mental image of a snarling dog, a fence, and a little girl when I prayed for healing of the memories for a friend. I asked her what this image meant to her. She said she had been extremely frightened by a dog when she was very young. While playing one day her pet dog had become trapped in a fence. In fear and pain he struggled violently against the wire mesh that entrapped him. As she tried to free him, he bit her coat and tore it. She could remember screaming until someone came to her rescue and took her coat out of the dog's mouth. Thus the fear and dislike of dogs had remained with her. The Lord healed that memory and completely took away all her fear. In fact, she purchased a dog for her son a short time after having prayer for inner healing.

On another occasion, the Holy Spirit revealed a mental "picture" of a lake with a large log on the edge of the bank that extended out into the water. When I asked the young lady what this picture meant to her, she remembered being at a lake with her family when she was just a toddler. Her frisky, inquisitive, little dog ran the full length of the log which jutted out into the water. The dog slipped on some mossy slime and fell into the water. She dashed toward the log to rescue him. When her mother saw this small child headed toward deep water, she began screaming, "Don't go near the water! Don't go near the water!" Her mother's extreme fear that she would fall in and drown was indelibly imprinted in the child's mind. At that moment, Satan saw his chance, and the fear of water entered her. All her life she had been afraid of water.

In both instances, the children were not physically harmed, but Satan used these situations to put fears into the hearts of young, innocent children. Those fears followed them into adulthood. In all of us is an inner child of the past.

If you have an abnormal fear concerning something, ask Jesus to reveal when that fear entered. Then, visualize Jesus in that situation. Ask Him to relive that situation with you, to take away the fear associated with it, and to heal your memory of that traumatic experience.

For example: When you visualize Jesus in a situation you simply claim the promise that Jesus is the same yesterday, today, and forever. (Hebrews 13:8) My husband, Ed, had an experience with this type of healing that will show what is meant by visualizing Jesus in a situation. I asked him to write his experience.

"Since 1962 I had been afraid of heights. I can identify the exact day on which this fear entered my life. We were on a trip to New York and other east coast cities with our family. We had taken our two young sons with us. The day we visited the top of the Empire State Building was a day when thunder showers were in the area. It had just rained and the wind was still blowing about 20 to 30 miles per hour. As we got to the top of the building our six year old son ran out of the elevator and started climbing the fence at the top of the building to get a better view of the city. I had not been watching him as closely as I should have and turned around to see him about three feet up the fence and still climbing. Uncontrollable fear and panic gripped me as I realized he might reach the top and be blown over the fence. I rushed to him, pulled him down, and spanked him soundly for scaring me this way. My knees were like rubber and would not function as they should all the time we were at the top of the building. From that date any time I was in a high place my knees would become shaky, and my head would become light as if I would faint. This acrophobia stayed with me for the next ten years.

At a prayer retreat the speaker told about introducing Jesus into a situation in our past to heal the fear or other intense emotion that had entered at that incident. I didn't really believe that it would work but was willing to try it. Her instructions were to relax and visualize the situation exactly as it happened, then to turn the situation over to Jesus and watch as He handled it for you. I leaned back in the chair and visualized the incident at the top of the Empire State Building. However, this time as I turned to see my son climbing the fence, I turned to Jesus who was standing beside me and said, "Jesus, will you take care of my son for me?" In my mind I watched as Jesus went quietly over and lifted my son from the fence. There was no spanking, no fear. Then Jesus took his hand and they walked around the top of the Empire State Building looking at the city and the sky. All fear left me and it was very peaceful.

Now I find that I can climb ladders, look off tall buildings, walk across swinging bridges, and do other things that would have brought the weakness in my knees and the lightheaded feeling previously. Jesus took an incident that was a horrible memory and changed it into a beautiful memory ten years after it happened. I have tried it with other incidents and find that Jesus introduced into any situation can change it into a beautiful memory and make it something that will be a blessing. In this incident Satan had taken a perfectly normal fear (concern for the safety of my son) and turned it into a uncontrollable fear that tormented me in many situations of my life. Satan often does this to us and causes us to be controlled by our fears. Jesus is our victory and we can defeat Satan if we will introduce Jesus into all situations in our life. Even if the situation is already past and the fear has had control, Jesus can change the ending if we will allow Him to."

Some Trauma Comes **Before** Birth or **Prior** to Conscious Memory—

The Bible tells us that John the Baptist leapt in Elizabeth's womb when she heard Mary's greeting. Psychologists believe that a baby can feel rejection, anxiety, and fear before it is born. If an unborn baby reacts to the nicotine that goes into his blood stream as his mother smokes, if a baby can be born with alcohol in its blood stream, and if a baby can be born addicted

22

to dope because his mother was taking dope—then it is scientifically plausible that the child could be affected in the emotional areas as well.

One day as I knelt with a friend and prayed for the healing of memories, the Holy Spirit revealed a mental image of a gray and white cat standing on his hind feet with front claws outstretched. The cat was snarling and hissing. I stopped praying and told her what the Holy Spirit had revealed. I asked her if she had been frightened as a child by a cat or if she was afraid of cats. She assured me that she loved cats. Later, when she mentioned the incident, her mother said, "When I was pregnant with you, I visited a relative who jokingly pitched a gray and white cat on me. The cat dug his claws in as he landed on my stomach and literally ripped my new maternity dress all the way down the front." The experience with this snarling cat was horrifying to the mother. The fear she felt apparently had been transmitted to the unborn baby. Through the years this lady had no conscious fear of cats, but prayer for the healing of memories revealed fear buried deep inside.

I was praying for another woman, and as I asked Jesus to heal her even as she was in her mother's womb, I felt such an overwhelming sense of rejection, loneliness, and sadness. It was such a devastating feeling. The lady started weeping and shared that she had been illegitimate. Her mother had told her many times as she was growing up how unwanted she had been. The Holy Spirit was revealing that even before she was born, she felt that horrible feeling of rejection.

Even before we are old enough to recall, our mind records in our subconscious (our memory bank) every fear or traumatic experience. My husband and I were praying for the healing of memories of a precious Indian girl. When I reached the age of 1 to 2 in her life and asked Jesus to heal any hurts at that age, I found I had a hard time breathing. I experienced a suffocating sensation. Ed had to pray for me before I could continue to pray for the girl. Her adopted mother shared later that the girl was born in a hogan on an Indian reservation. Shortly after birth, she contracted tuberculosis and almost died before the age of two. The Holy Spirit had revealed to me that this girl had suffered the fear and agony of not being able to breathe deeply when she was just a baby. We believe that the Lord removed

23

that deep, hidden fear of suffocation and death from her subconscious.

Cathering Marshall, in **Something More,** says:

We are accustomed to the idea that we pass on to our children a physical inheritance—color of eyes, color of hair, even certain diseases: tendencies toward gout, diabetes, certain skin diseases. Handing down a material inheritance is such standard practice that the laws of every country make careful provisions governing wills, probate, death and inheritances taxes. I began to ask myself, is it possible that our spiritual inheritance is as real as the others?

It soon became apparent that just as we can inherit either a fortune or debts, so in the spiritual realm we can inherit either spiritual blessings or those liabilities (unabashedly called "sins" in Scripture) that hinder our development into mature persons. These blessings or liabilities do not come to us solely by heredity. Obviously they are also passed on by example and by teaching—conscious or unconscious.

Some May Need Inner Healing for **Deep** Hurts Because of—
WHO YOU ARE

Perhaps you were born into a family where you were unwanted and unloved. You may have been the "wrong" sex and you grew up feeling your parents' disappointment because you were not the "boy" they wanted or the "girl" they had planned on. Were you one of many children, and your parents found it difficult to take care of another child? Were you raised in a home where there was constant bickering and fighting? Did you have an alcoholic parent? Were you always blamed and criticized as a child and never allowed to forget your mistakes? Were you constantly compared to someone else and his achievements? Did your family always have negative attitudes instead of positive attitudes?

One lovely lady grew up in a home full of criticism and negative attitudes. Each person was always compared to another; their achievements were belittled instead of praised. She had been completely burdened down with a life full of this negativism. Now she was miserable and badly in need of help. At the close of the meeting, when I was ministering, she came

24

up for prayer. She was crying so hard she could barely talk. Since there was not time for deep counseling, we agreed on a later appointment. When we met she spoke of the many strained and broken relationships in her family. Her mother always had such a negative attitude, and this lady felt she had developed the same negative outlook on life. "Is there something more to life than this?" she asked.

First, I made sure that she knew Jesus as her personal Savior. Then as we knelt by the sofa, I asked Jesus to set her free from all those negative forces—inferiority, lack of confidence, timidity, etc. Then I asked Jesus to fill her with positive forces, positive thoughts, to fill her mouth with praises, to put a glow on her face, joy in her heart, to baptize her in His love. He did just that! Instantly there was a new radiance about her.

Within a short time she shared this new dimension of Jesus with her family and they saw how He had transformed her mind—her life. When I see that family today my spirit just soars. The lovely mother and two beautiful daughters glow with joy and happiness and the love of Jesus. The mother is filled with confidence and assurance and a new boldness to witness for her Lord.

Perhaps you may need inner healing for hurts because someone said you were just like a certain member of your family; maybe this person was mean or disliked. If your parents were divorced, your mother may have reminded you that you would probably grow up to be just like your dad, and you knew what she thought of him. He was a failure who had failed and deserted the family. You may need inner healing because you were teased as a child about your size, your looks, your race, your poverty. "Teasing" is wrong and hurtful, whether it is done by an adult or child.

You may have lost a parent through death or were separated from your parents because of illness or divorce, and you felt such loneliness and rejection. So many children are beaten or molested, and they grow up with the terror and the horror of this injustice. If you did not feel loved as a child, you may not be able to show love to others, and you may not be able to accept yourself. It may even affect your relationship with God, and perhaps you will find yourself not being able to love Him as you want or should.

One of the most heartbreaking stories I have ever heard is the story of a 17-year-old boy whom we will call "J". He was brought to us by his adopted mother. When he came, he would barely look us in the eye; he sat over in the chair looking downcast, dejected. This is his story as he shared it with us. His own mother had been an alcoholic; he did not know who his father was. There were three other brothers; each had a different father. He had been beaten, neglected, unloved. He grew up feeling completely rejected. Being the oldest, he had assumed the responsibility of trying to care for his three younger brothers. On occasions, he even had to eat from garbage cans.

Before Ed and I started praying for this 17-year-old, we made certain that he knew Jesus as his personal Savior. Ed asked the Holy Spirit to reveal what "giants" Satan had sent against him. We prayed for God's protection and then we asked Jesus to set this boy free from Satan's bondage. There were so many negative forces keeping him in bondage: schizophrenia, fears, depression, oppression, rejection, resentment, suicide, bitterness, confusion, and others. We claimed Matthew 18:18 ". . . Whatever you bind on earth is bound in heaven, and whatever you free on earth will be freed in heaven." After "J" had renounced all the forces that Satan had sent against him, we asked Jesus to fill the void completely with His love, His joy, His peace, and to fill "J" completely with His presence and the presence of the Holy Spirit.

The Lord led me to pray for healing of memories from the time before birth up to the present. As I reached the years between four and five, the Holy Spirit revealed a mental image of a little boy over in a corner with his hands protecting his head as if he were trying to ward off blows. I stopped praying and asked "J" what this image meant. He said, "that was my most painful memory." He could remember his mother and the man she was living with yelling and arguing. The man kept saying, "Get rid of him; he's not mine. Get rid of him; he's not mine." Those words kept ringing in "J's" ears all his young life, tormenting him.

But let me tell you what the healing power of Jesus did. The Lord touched "J" and for over one hour he literally was under the power of the Lord. "J" was filled with the Holy Spirit and the Lord healed all those hurts, those painful memories, and set him free from bondage. Our parting that night was memorable. "J" was out on the porch when he suddenly turned, came back, very hesitantly leaned down and gave me a hug. The healing process, being able to show love to others, had already begun.

Two years later that young man's life revealed the miracle of God's redeeming love and grace. He graduated from high school and his adoptive mother had been told by counselors that he wouldn't be able to make it emotionally or mentally. Of course, Satan still comes against him at times, but "J" has learned that Satan is a defeated foe. "J" knows that He that is in him is greater than he that is in the world. (See 1 John 4:4 KJV) We can never praise the Lord enough for what He did for this young man. A year after inner healing he preached a forty-five minute sermon in his own church. Thank you, Jesus, for the miracles You performed in "J's" life.

You May Need Inner Healing Because Of—
WHAT YOU HAVE DONE

You may have committed a crime and you are overcome by shame and disgrace. Some people are behind real prison bars; other people are in prisons within their own minds. Both prisons are devastating. You may have inflicted deep hurt on a mate or distressed your parents terribly. They have since died and you feel there is no way you can seek their forgiveness or make restitution for the pain you caused them. Some of you, before accepting Jesus, lived a life filled with sin, corruption and immorality. You know the Lord has forgiven you for your past sins, because He says, ". . . I will never again remember their sins and lawless deeds" (Hebrews 10:17), but you cannot forgive yourself. Your past memories plague you. If guilt and condemnation have you completely bowed down, Satan is the one who sends that condemnation. The Bible says "God did not send his Son into the world to condemn it, but to save it." (John 3:17) Cecil Osborne wrote in **The Art of Understanding Yourself,** "Guilt, whether real or false, can be handled in only two ways. It must be forgiven or punished. If we cannot secure forgiveness, we find a way to punish ourselves physically, mentally, or circumstantially—."

A young married woman named Rita* came for prayer. Thoughts of suicide plagued her. Her marriage was crumbling. She was not living an abundant, joyful life, even though she professed to be a Christian. During prayer for inner healing, the Holy Spirit revealed a strong spirit of guilt connected with the death of someone. I stopped praying and told her what the Holy Spirit had revealed. Her face clouded over with grief, her muscles tensed, and she confessed that she felt she had caused her dad's death. Her father died when she was ten. A few days before he died, in childish anger she had shouted, "I hate you, I wish you were dead." Her father did die unexpectedly within the week.

This child had grown up feeling that somehow her angry remarks had caused her father's death. All these years Satan had deceived her with false guilt. She grew up with such a negative attitude that she found it extremely difficult to relate positively to anyone. Now she was unable to love herself, her family, or her husband. She had never been able to accept God's forgiveness for these feelings of false guilt. The last time we heard from Rita, she was in a psychiatric hospital, broken in mind and body.

I recall another young lady I will call Carmen who came for prayer who had deep, deep guilt that was not **false**—but **real guilt.** Hurt after hurt had left such horrible feelings of rejection. She had a physical deformity which made her feel so unlovely, so unloved. She was completely bowed down with remorse and shame and was miserable. Her body shook with sobs and the tears literally flooded down her face.

She shared how she had been promiscuous as a teenager and faced the embarrassment and shame of giving birth to an illegitimate child. Her heart still ached as she told how she gave her baby up for adoption. But through the healing power of Jesus and with the sword of the Spirit those chains of guilt were cut from her and she was free at last to accept God's forgiveness. The Lord instantly transformed her through inner healing. Her family could see God's transformation in her life the moment she came home.

Carmen was able to **accept** God's forgiveness for **real** guilt

---

* Name has been changed.

and was set free, whereas Rita **could not accept** God's forgiveness even for **false** guilt and was kept in bondage. Not all God's inner healings are instantaneous, or so visibly evident, but when they are it is beautiful and glorious.

We have prayed with many people who have been involved in the occult; I want to share some of the stories with you. One lady was deeply involved in reincarnation and Edgar Cayce. She took astrology courses and learned how to plot horoscopes. She had gone to a medium, taken yoga, played with ouija boards, and studied hypnotism. She said, "just name it and I have been involved in it." And all the time she had been teaching a Sunday School class. She even took her books on a "Sleeping Prophet" to her minister, the pastor of a large, thriving, liberal church and asked if they were O.K. His answer was, "I see no harm in them." Actually, she was earnestly searching for God and His truths, but this avenue only led her away from God. While this young lady had everything in life money could buy, she was not happy. She was obsessed with a deep fear of death concerning her children and frightened by an even stronger spirit of self-destruction.

We bound Satan in the name of Jesus and had her renounce everything involving the occult. Then we prayed, asking Jesus to set her free from all the fears Satan had sent against her, from the spirit of self-destruction, etc. We asked Jesus to fill the void, to repair the damage that had been done by seeking knowledge from Satan instead of from God. Finally we asked the Lord to heal every hurt or painful memory. This young lady said she felt as if a mighty weight had been lifted from her shoulders. Later she said, "You know, two hours in prayer asking the Lord to heal and cleanse is better than ten years of psychiatry." Praise the Lord! He completely set her free from all oppression. Today she is constantly working for the Lord in a hospital ministry, visiting the sick and sharing Jesus.

Another lady we prayed with said that her mother had been involved in seances and ESP and that she had inherited the same ESP powers. She confided that at times she felt as if she were going out of her mind. Three years earlier she accepted Jesus as Savior and had renounced the occult, but she was still having problems and she kept doubting her salvation. She would cry and cry as Satan would torment and deceive her.

There were times she was unable to say the name Jesus. During these times we kept pleading the blood of Jesus and binding Satan in the name of Jesus until finally she was able to utter the life-giving name, **JESUS.** I prayed with her over the phone several times and Ed and I prayed with her personally for inner healing. When we saw her later, she had a beautiful glow on her face and said she felt great—free from Satan's oppression. Encounters with the occult always bring fear and unrest. Only Jesus brings peace.

The wife of one couple who came for prayer also had been very involved in reincarnation, pendulum swinging, etc. She confessed that at times she had been miffed at her husband because he hadn't shown interest in all the books she was reading. (What was so tragic was that in two of the above cases, the ladies had attended seminars at their own churches where the speakers had believed in reincarnation.) This precious wife was horrified to learn that the Lord considered the occult a sin. (Deuteronomy 18:10-11) ". . . no Israeli may practice black magic, or call on the evil spirits for aid, or be a fortune teller, or be a serpent charmer, medium, or wizard, or call forth the spirits of the dead."

Immediately she renounced all aspects of the occult and asked the Lord's forgiveness. When they returned home, she and her husband made a huge bonfire and they burned over one hundred dollars worth of books on the occult. To see this couple today is such a blessing. They both shine with the glory of the Lord on them. Thank you, Lord, that through Your healing power and through inner healing, these people found the peace in You that they were searching for.

One lady from another city who had requested prayer telephoned to ask if she could bring a member of her family with her. When the husband and wife arrived, they were accompanied by a young man with a full beard and an unkempt appearance.

The conversation soon disclosed that the young man had just been released from a hospital in another state where he had been treated for drug addiction. He had been in the drug traffic and some of his friends were well-known criminals in a penitentiary. He was very uncomfortable when anything about Jesus was mentioned. Each time the conversation turned to spiritual things he would switch the subject back to his father and what his father had done to him. He had extreme hatred for his father. Ed asked him if we could pray with him for healing of memories.

As we knelt down by our sofa to pray, we felt a check concerning the young man's salvation even though he had been a church member. Ed offered the prayer for salvation and had him repeat the date and the time so that there could be no question concerning his having asked Jesus to save him. As we started into the prayer for inner healing, the Holy Spirit revealed to Ed that the young man had been involved in Satan worship. Then we noticed a gold ring on his finger in the form of a snake. Ed asked him to take it off and to renounce Satan and repeat out loud, "Satan, I will no longer serve you and I renounce you and all your power over me." Ed had a feeling that he also had something around his neck that was a symbol of his worship of Satan. He assured us that he did not have anything around his neck. Then the Holy Spirit revealed that he had been a priest in the worship of Satan. He confessed that he had and Ed asked him to repeat this statement, "I break all vows and agreements that have been made between myself and Satan and ask forgiveness for my involvement with Satan."

We prayed together asking the Holy Spirit to reveal all the forces that Satan had sent against him. Rejection, rebellion, loneliness, hatred, and laziness were some of the strong forces that were controlling him. Ed took authority over these forces in the name of Jesus and commanded them to leave him. Then we prayed asking Jesus to walk back through his memories to heal all the hurts and scars from his hatred of his father and from the other things in his past.

The results of this prayer were not immediately apparent. There was no show of emotion, no great change in his countenance. We felt that even though the Lord had done **His** part, the young man's rebellion and hatred were still so strong that not much had changed. The Holy Spirit continued to work in his life and one week later he was in church for the first time in a number of years. He told his brother-in-law that he could not understand how Ed knew about the symbol he usually wore around his neck. It was the symbol of the ram's head with ruby red eyes, the symbol of this young man's devotion to

Satan. That night was the first time he had not worn this symbol. He removed the snake ring and has not worn it or the ram's head since. We are trusting the Lord to continue to work in his life. Since, He that is in us is greater than he that is in the world, we are praying for a complete victory in that life. This young man has great potential and could be such a strong witness for Jesus. His sister is a beautiful, radiant Christian filled with the Holy Spirit. The Lord has used her and her Spirit-filled husband to win many of their family to the Lord. They have touched numerous lives in the city where they live.

You May Need Inner Healing Because Of—
WHERE YOU HAVE BEEN

Have you ever been in a terrifying accident—or even a near accident that left emotional scars? We were enjoying the fellowship of another couple one night when the husband mentioned that he almost had 30 to 40 wrecks over the last twenty years. Every time he got into the car, he would become very sleepy; many times he had fallen asleep at the wheel. He would be off the road in the ditch or down the side of a freeway embankment when he awoke. This man was a happily married, Spirit-filled Christian who did **not** drink. Doctors had checked him to see if they could find the reason for this problem but there was no medical explanation.

As we discussed his problem, the Holy Spirit dropped into my mind, "this is a spirit of slumber." I shared this with him. He said, "Would you and Ed pray with me about this?" So my husband and I prayed for him. While we were praying, the Holy Spirit showed me a mental picture of a car with a black mass hovering over it and revealed that the black mass represented death. When I asked what this meant to him, he said, "I have no idea." So, we asked the Holy Spirit to reveal to him what this meant. No answer came immediately, but later, as we were having pie and coffee, the man said excitedly, "I remember what it was!"

"Twenty years ago, I was driving a car-load of boys back to the Army camp. We were in danger of being late, and I was driving fast. I passed one car, and the car behind me started to go around the same car, but there was not enough time and it was involved in a head-on collision with a truck coming over the hill. I wanted to stop, and yet, I couldn't, or we'd be AWOL at camp. The news was in the paper the next day; all the occupants in the other car had been killed." Satan had deceived him all these years into thinking that somehow **he** had caused the wreck. He felt such guilt and condemnation for an accident that was in no way his fault, and under the circumstances could he be blamed for not stopping to try to help. Psychologists would say that by his falling asleep in the car, he was trying to blot out the painful memory and the feeling of **false guilt** about the accident. Jesus did in one second what medical science had not been able to do. He completely blotted out the feeling of false guilt and condemnation. A year has passed, and this man has not fallen asleep one time in the car. He called recently to report that he had driven more than 1,100 miles in two days and had not fallen asleep or even become drowsy. In fact, the extreme drowsiness has left him completely. Praise the Lord!

This man's wife came later for inner healing. There were no serious problems but she felt so inadequate and inferior. She was filled with fear and self-consciousness. The Lord completely took away all that bondage. This once shy person, who lacked self-confidence, is now boldly and confidently teaching Bible classes and is the prayer chairman for a large group of Christian women.

Perhaps you have suffered a mental breakdown and have undergone shock treatments in a psychiatric hospital. One lady who was brought to us at a retreat had suffered a mental breakdown. She was a Christian, a lovely, intelligent person. Her husband had been extremely ill, and she had been under tremendous stress during his illness. When he recovered, she collapsed mentally and physically. During the time of her depression and mental illness, her husband filed divorce proceedings against her. One can imagine the feelings of rejection, bitterness, anger, and self-pity that would be sent against you by Satan at a time like this. She had been taking numerous tranquilizers each day. In fact, that morning she had already taken several.

When we prayed for healing of her memories, we asked Jesus to fill her with the Holy Spirit and to fill her with His love, joy, and peace. Instantly, Jesus touched her by His power, and it was as if a veil had been lifted from her face. The effects of the drugs were gone; the depression was gone, and Jesus filled her with His joy. Her face was aglow with His love; there was a twinkle in her eyes. She had arthritis of the knee and had been having it treated each week to have the fluid removed. The Lord healed her arthritic knee and even took away the "squeak" in her knees.

You may have been involved in a traumatic and terrifying experience, and the horror and terror is still so real you wake up at night with agonizing nightmares. Perhaps you have gone through bankruptcy or a financial upheaval, and you are overcome with a sense of despair and futility. Maybe you have just gone through the agony of losing a loved one through death or a mate through divorce. You may have deep scars from sorrow and grief. Jesus wants to heal your scars.

Early one Monday morning, a mother brought her eight-year-old daughter to our home for prayer. They were both precious, Southern Baptist, Spirit-filled Christians. This is the mother's story. Just one month before, her 14-year-old son had been horribly burned in a freakish accident. He had started to mow the lawn, moments later, they heard someone pounding on the door. Judy, the eight-year-old sister, went to open the door, and there was Gary with flames engulfing the top part of his body. As the mother tried to put out the flames, his skin fell off in her hands. He was rushed to the hospital where he lived only a few days. The night before he died, he had a glorious experience with the Lord. He called his daddy into the room and said, "Dad, I've just accepted Jesus as my Savior." He lifted his burned arms and sang praises to the Lord. The next morning, he went to be with Jesus.

The little sister could not get over the grief, the horror, of the tragedy. Each thought of her brother's death sent her into hysterics; her little body would become rigid with fear and terror. Nightmares kept her from sleeping; she wasn't eating. She was pathetically in need of help. First, we prayed for the child, binding Satan and all his evil spirits in the mighty name of Jesus. Then we asked Jesus to walk back into her memory of that terrifying experience and to take a spiritual eraser and wipe away the terror and horror. We asked Him to heal the hurt, to heal her broken heart, and to heal her mind. We then prayed the same prayer for the mother.

The mother had found it very difficult to forgive God for taking her son. She was in a state of rebellion toward Him. But that morning God's emcompassing love filled her heart and she said, "Oh! God I forgive you, I forgive you for allowing this accident to happen. I forgive you for letting Gary die." Then she added through her sobs, "Lord forgive me for my resentment and rebellion toward you." Glory came down at that moment and filled the room and their hearts.

The Lord touched them both by His mighty power. Jesus instantly gave this little girl a spirit of joy and peace. Then, the most glorious thing happened. Our gracious Lord gave the mother a vision of Gary walking hand-in-hand with Jesus. As she described the beautiful vision of heaven with its vivid green trees and shining river, we could almost see it ourselves. Gary, in her vision, was completely whole. All the burned areas of his body had been completely healed, and his hair had all grown back. His ears were back on. The mother was given such peace, such joy, that she said, "Oh! I wouldn't bring Gary back to this earth even if I could." As the mother was sharing this vision, the glory of the Lord was on both her and her daughter. Judy, in a bubbly voice, said, "Mother, was Gary going fishing with Jesus in that beautiful river? Mother, was Peter there going fishing with them, too?"

The presence of the Lord was so real during this time, words cannot describe the experience. We just praised His name and sang songs of joy, and thanked Him for His goodness and love. They have shared this testimony with many people, and it has changed so many lives. At one prayer meeting when they shared their story, fifteen people accepted Jesus as their Savior. Our prayer is that the Lord will constantly minister to this precious family, to bless them and continue to heal their broken hearts. We claim God's promise in Psalms 147:3 for each member of this family—"He heals the broken-hearted, binding up their wounds."

All of us need inner healing in some way or another. Jesus is waiting for us to let Him heal all our painful memories, hurts, fears, disappointments. It doesn't matter if the painful memory is an old, old hurt or a new wound, He wants to start the healing process. He wants to go all the way back to the **root** problem and cleanse and heal us completely. Not only does God want to **heal** our mind, He wants to **renew** our mind!

Chapter IV

God Wants You To Be Whole

(Spirit, Soul, and Body)

The emphasis of this book is not on physical healing nor on spiritual healing as such, but on inner healing. It is simply a testimony of our own experiences in intercessory prayer for inner healing and healing of memories. However, there have been times when the Lord, through His redemptive love, performed all three types of healing in one person: **spiritual, physical,** and **inner healing.**

Spiritual Healing
(Spirit)

The story of a girl we will call Ann is a beautiful example of the Lord's healing a person in all three areas. Ann was an adopted baby. Later, her adoptive parents were divorced. When she was 13, her mother remarried, but Ann did not have a pleasant relationship with her step father. In her teen years, she tried almost everything that Satan had to offer. She married early and had a baby that was diagnosed as having cerebral palsy. (The Lord later healed the baby.) Her husband was in a car accident that left his brain damaged. This marriage ended in divorce. Her mother became ill and died in her arms.

Imagine one person having so many horrible and traumatic experiences.

When we first met, her face reflected total rejection, despair, rebellion, resentment, fear and hatred. She was sick in mind and body. One thing had been in her favor. She had gone to live with foster parents, and through them, had found the Lord as her personal Savior. They brought her to us for inner healing. The Lord had already done a remarkable work in her life spiritually, and she had received spiritual healing, but she was still in bondage because of her wrong attitudes and painful memories.

We prayed that she would be able to reclaim the inheritance that was rightfully hers—righteousness, peace and joy. We took authority over Satan in the name of Jesus and had her renounce the negative forces he had sent against her— rejection, resentment, bitterness, hatred, etc. We asked Jesus to fill the void with His love, His peace and His joy, with forgiveness. We asked the Lord to heal her mind, her emotions. Then we prayed asking Jesus to heal her many painful memories.

Praise the Lord, not only did the Lord begin inner healing, but when the power of the Lord came over her, she was instantly healed of a hernia. The presence of the Holy Spirit was so strong she and I barely could walk out of the room. Complete inner healing with Ann was gradual and progressive, but months later, to look at her it would be difficult to recognize her because of the dramatic change. In one heartwarming story we see the mercy of God in three types of healing—spiritual, inner, and physical.

I am reminded of another girl who was healed of inner scars and at the same time, God removed a physical scar from her shoulder as well. I prayed for this twenty-four year old girl who had always had a mental block concerning reading. Also, she felt that something was keeping her from being completely free from growing with the Lord as she wanted. Because she was an intelligent girl, the parents had taken her to a psychologist, reading specialists, and speech therapists during her younger years in an effort to discover the source of her reading disability. Before prayer for inner healing we had her renounce the different negative forces Satan had sent against her.

She shared that she had been severely burned when she was very young. She did not give the age, but when I was praying for the healing of her memories, the Holy Spirit revealed the exact age at which the tragic accident occurred—she was two years old. When we got to that time in her life, she started weeping profusely. She had assumed that this painful and traumatic memory had been healed long ago, but Satan had kept it buried way down deep inside of her. I did not know where she had been burned or that she had scars but when she started crying, I touched her shoulder to comfort her. She later said that I placed my hand exactly on the burned scar.

She called back after she returned home to say that the warmth of the Holy Spirit had remained all the way home. She and her mother examined her shoulder and the Lord had removed almost all the twenty-two year old scar. What was so beautiful was the fact that not only did Jesus set her free from bondage and heal the inner scars and painful memories, but He also removed the outer scars where she had been burned. She felt as if that day the mental blockage in reading had been partially removed. Even on the way home she found it much easier to read the signs on the side of the road.

Sometimes Satan will hide a painful memory way down deep in the darkest recesses of our mind. The "hidden" memory will cause physical ailments or emotional problems, but we won't know why we are having the problems or when the problem began. When we ask Jesus to walk into our past and heal the painful memories, when we give our hurts over to Him, so often we are healed physically also.

Physical healing is only one side of the triangle of divine healing—and it is so beautiful. As someone has said there is no "small" healing, if you are in pain and the Lord heals you—to you it is important, exciting and wonderful.

The New Testament is filled with miracles of Jesus healing the sick. He touched the blind and they saw. He touched the crippled and they walked. He touched the diseased and they were healed. We read in 1 Peter 2:24 ". . . For his wounds have healed ours!" Jesus tells us ". . . anyone believing in me shall do the same miracles I have done, and even greater ones, because I am going to be with the Father. . ." (John 14:12-13) Jesus made these promises and we can trust Him and believe that He wants us to pray for the sick, in faith believing that they shall be healed. The last part of the great commission says, ". . . they will be able to place their hands on the sick and heal them." (Mark 16:18).

Joy wells up inside of me when I think of a friend's mother who had been on a breathing machine for two years for a lung condition and the Lord healed her instantly. I really want to leap for joy when I think of the lady from Florida who was instantly healed of a terribly painful hernia. One year later she returned to Houston and told us her healing had been verified by her doctor. A lady from Mississippi who was healed of glaucoma also visited in Houston a year after the Lord touched her eyes and was praising Him that her doctor had verified her healing.

How thrilling it was when the Lord healed a man in the emergency room of a hospital where he was taken after having a heart attack. The man said, "I know why the Lord spared me that Saturday morning, it was for me to share Jesus. Four people accepted Christ after I told them about the Lord healing me." How do you explain how the Lord dissolves growths or straightens eyes? There is no way—we just praise Him. All things are possible through prayer! We watched in amazement as the Lord lengthened my own little grandmother's leg two and one-half inches right before our eyes in our own home. She had suffered a broken hip years before and the thigh bone was pushed up into the hip socket. She walks without a limp now.

Ed and I rejoice and stand in awe when we think of the lady with the serious heart problem who was on her way to the hospital that very night when she came by our house with a friend for prayer. The Lord instantly healed her and she did not go to the hospital. (She had been on daily medication and had missed a tremendous amount of work because of severe fibrillation of the heart.) A year later she still feels great. We want to shout "Praise the Lord" when we think of the lady who stood in proxy for a friend who was in pain as she recovered from surgery. In the process of praying for another, her own heart problem was healed.

A question frequently raised is, "Why aren't all people healed when they are prayed for?" Only God knows the answer to that question. Apparently, there are certain conditions that must be met. Cecil Osborne in **The Art of Understanding Yourself** says, "If there are inner conflicts and tensions, anxiety and guilt at some point in his life, the individual will tend to manifest this spiritual disease by some physical symptom."

If deep resentment has caused a person to have ulcers and he cannot overcome this resentment, he may not be healed. (All ulcers, are not necessarily caused by resentment.) If extreme fear and worry has caused a heart problem and the person cannot overcome his fears, then it is doubtful that the Lord will heal him. Why should the Lord heal a person of a lung condition if he continues to smoke many packs of cigarettes every day? Or why should He heal a person with a diseased liver if he continues to drink enormous amounts of liquor?

We can justify, in a way, why people are not healed when they insist on harming their bodies, but the question is asked, "What about the person who has walked hand-in-hand with the Lord in a beautiful Spirit-filled walk, has the faith to move mountains, and yet, is not healed . . . Why, Lord?" Apparently, our faith (or lack of faith) is not the only criteria for being healed.

Catherine Marshall, in her book, **Something More,** wrote that when her granddaughter was born with serious birth defects, the family decided to pray in faith and ask for a miraculous healing. People gathered for days of intense prayer, but Amy Catherine died after only six weeks of life. Catherine Marshall recovered from this deep, agonizing hurt when she was finally able to pray the prayer of relinquishment and then to go one step further and praise the Lord in the midst of the circumstance. She says concerning her own illness in 1943, "God would not allow me to get well until I saw Him even in my illness. Disease is of Satan's kingdom, but God allowed it for me. Blame it on Satan, I might, but see God in it, I must."

We must release each person to the Lord. We cannot "box" God in. It is not our objective to try to figure out why some are healed and some are not. Not everyone will accept Jesus as his personal Savior, but we must keep on sharing the Good News of Jesus. Not everyone is physically healed the way we expect, but we must continue praying and lifting the sick up to our Father for His highest. His highest may be to heal them on earth, or it may be to heal them in Heaven. Our calling is to pray, relinquish, and praise.

The greatest healing is **spiritual healing** (salvation). "For God loved the world so much that he gave his only Son so that anyone who believes in him shall not perish but have eternal life. God did not send his Son into the world to condemn it, but to save it." (John 3:16-17) Many people cannot believe that God will forgive and forget, or that He really means it when He says, ". . . I will never again remember their sins and lawless deeds." (Hebrew 10:17) Salvation is the foundation from which all other healing comes. It is because of the shed blood of Jesus on the cross that we can have complete cleansing and healing.

Spiritual healing can be described in one word— FORGIVENESS. This involves receiving God's forgiveness for our sins, and then forgiving those who have sinned against us.

For spiritual cleansing and healing from our sins, we must:

1. Confess our sins and ask forgiveness from Jesus.

2. Forgive those who have sinned against us.

3. Invite Jesus into our heart to become our personal Savior.

4. Turn from sin and ask Jesus to take control of our life.

Almost the first thing we ask when counseling with someone is, "Have you invited Jesus into your heart as your Lord and Savior?" Sometimes an individual will seem vague, or perhaps he will say, "Well, I've been in church all of my life," or "I am a Christian because I was sprinkled as a baby," or "Yes, my mother always took me to church." But just doing all these things does not make a person a Christian. Then very gently we ask, "Do you know Jesus as your own personal Savior?" "Have you ever confessed your sins and taken Him into your heart?" If the answer is no, or they are unsure, we always have them repeat the sinner's prayer and ask Jesus to come into their hearts.

Among those healed spiritually was the husband of a young schoolteacher. When she made an appointment for counseling, she said, "My husband calls himself an agnostic; we are not in church, but I want all the Lord has to offer. I want to be completely filled with the Holy Spirit." When she arrived that night I looked over her shoulder and there was her husband. He had driven her over, and then, very reluctantly, agreed to come inside with her.

He listened as we told her of our love for Jesus and of all the ways He had shown His love for us. Just at the right moment, the Holy Spirit impressed me, now is the time to stop talking and start praying. Turning to her I said, "The Lord wants us to pray with you." Still under the Spirit's guidance I turned to her agnostic husband and asked if he would like for us to pray with him also? To our amazement, he said, "Yes." So, praise the Lord, my husband and I knelt by the sofa with him. Ed led him to pray the sinner's prayer to receive Jesus as his Savior and then we prayed for inner healing. We asked Jesus to fill him with the Holy Spirit. He did! Later we prayed with his wife (the one who had asked for prayer in the first place). These two schoolteachers left arm in arm praising the Lord. Since that night they have grown in the Lord and are walking with Him daily.

There is no greater joy than to lead someone to the Lord!

As I have said before, **Spiritual Healing** is the most significant and important healing. **Physical Healing** is glorious; but we can be Christians, in good physical condition and still be miserable and be an emotional cripple. It is through **Inner Healing,** through healing of memories that the other side of the divine triangle of divine healing is made complete. It is so vital, so necessary. Without inner peace, without healing of the soul **(mind),** we cannot be in perfect harmony with our Lord. God is so good—God wants us to be whole: Spirit, Soul, and Body.

Chapter V

Before You Pray for Inner Healing

Jesus knows everything about you, and He **still** loves you. He wants to give you life eternal. He wants to set you free from bondage. He wants to heal you physically. He wants to take away all your hurts. He wants to heal your emotional wounds. He wants to heal your mind, your painful memories. He wants you to be WHOLE. There are some things, though, that **you** must do before the Lord gives you that inner peace that comes through inner healing. God does His part, but He gives you the responsibility of doing your part, also. We have listed some of the conditions that must be met before a person can receive inner healing from God.

SALVATION

1 John 1:9 "But if we confess our sins to him, he can be depended on to forgive us and to cleanse us from every wrong . . ."

Romans 10:9 "For if you tell others with your own mouth that Jesus Christ is your Lord, and believe in your own heart that God has raised him from the dead, you will be saved."

The very first and most important requirement is to make certain you know Jesus as your personal Savior. Perhaps you have never invited Jesus into your heart as your Savior, or maybe you are a church member who still has doubts about your salvation. If a person is unsure that he is a Christian we usually ask this question, "If the Lord were to come right now, do you know without a shadow of a doubt you would go to be with him?" If you don't know, that you know, then by all means ask Jesus into your heart this very moment. Remember, the steps to salvation are: (a) confess your sins, (b) forgive others, (c) invite Jesus into your heart, and (d) turn completely from sin. We want you to say the following prayer. Even though you've repeated this prayer many times before, repeat it again—knowing that if you are truly repentant He is faithful and just to forgive your sins and to save you.

Prayer for Salvation

Lord Jesus, I know I am a sinner and have sinned. I confess my sins to you. I ask forgiveness of all my sins—those sins I remember and those sins I've forgotten about. I forgive those who have sinned against me.

Lord Jesus come into my heart as my Savior. I surrender my life to you. I make you Lord of my heart and life. I commit myself totally and completely to you. Thank you for coming into my heart as my personal Savior. I love you and want to serve you forever. Amen.

Now, I want you to write the date in your Bible when you committed your life to Christ. Then when Satan comes against you with doubts, you can say, "Satan, you are a liar and a deceiver, because on this very date written in my Bible, I asked forgiveness of my sins, asked Jesus into my heart and He is in my heart as Lord of my life."

RENOUNCE THE OCCULT AND CULTS

Leviticus 19:31 "Do not defile yourselves by consulting mediums and wizards, for I am Jehovah your God."

Deuteronomy 18:10-11 ". . . No Israeli may practice black magic, or call on the evil spirits for aid, or be a fortune teller, or be a serpent charmer, medium, or wizard, or call forth the spirits of the dead."

If you have been involved in the occult, either seriously or just for fun, you should renounce those things. Many people have sought peace and contentment from sources other than from God. To do this is an abomination to the Lord. We can get information from two places, from God or from Satan. God leads toward truth and enlightment, but information sought from any source other than from Him leads toward destruction.

The occult includes: reincarnation, astrology, horoscopes, ESP, seances, ouija boards, tarot cards, fortune telling, witchcraft, pendulum swinging, automatic writing, palm reading, etc. The cults include transcendental meditation, Eastern religions and other false religions.

All books and articles upholding the occult or cults should be destroyed. Ask the Lord to reveal to you, to bring to your rememberance those items you have that should be destroyed.

If you have had any involvement with the occult or cults, then pray this prayer asking for forgiveness and renounce Satan.

> Satan, I renounce you! I renounce the occult and the cults! I renounce any group or practice, or belief that does not glorify Jesus. I ask your forgiveness Jesus, for involvement with any of these things. Thank you for forgiving me, for cleansing me and for setting me free from the occult. It is in your name Jesus that I pray. Amen.

FORGIVENESS

> Matthew 6:14-15 "Your heavenly Father will forgive you if you forgive those who sin against you; but if **you** refuse to forgive **them, he** will not forgive **you.**"

> Matthew 5:24 ". . . leave your sacrifice there beside the alter and go and apologize and be reconciled to him . . ."

Unless, you are willing to forgive those who have hurt you, you will not be able to receive complete inner healing. You may say, "I was hurt so deeply, I don't think I can forgive." Then say, "Lord, I know I must forgive, I do want to forgive, but I cannot do it myself. Would You help me to forgive?" Give Jesus your will, and let Him forgive through you. Make the conscious decision, "Yes, I will forgive those who have hurt me." Take authority over the unforgiving spirit that Satan has sent against you, and ask Jesus to fill you with love and forgiveness. Don't forgive on conditions—"I'll forgive you if you stop drinking and gambling", or "I'll forgive her if she apologizes first," etc. We must forgive **unconditionally.**

I'm so aware that it is very easy for a counselor or minister to say to a person, "You must forgive," but it is another thing for that person who has been so horribly mistreated to be able to say, "Yes, I do forgive."

I have counseled with people and have been horrified at some of the sins committed against them. I've often wondered how they could even function as a normal human being after what they have been through.

I remember praying with one young person who had been raised in a home filled with depravity, sin and lust, and with her mother's knowledge, she had been repeatedly molested by a member of her family. No wonder she said, "I cannot forgive my mother or the person who molested me." When the hurt is still so deep that they cannot forgive, we as counselors must keep loving them. We must have enough faith for them too, and assure them that the time will come when the deep wounds will be healed and Christ's love and light will completely push out the darkness of Satan. As counselors we must not heap more condemnation on them because at that particular time they cannot say "I forgive." We must keep lifting them up in prayer until God's healing love fills them with a desire to forgive.

HONESTY

> Proverbs 12:5 "A good man's mind is filled with honest thoughts; an evil man's mind is crammed with lies."
>
> Proverbs 12:17 "A good man is known by his truthfulness; a false man by deceit and lies."

You must be completely honest with yourself, with the person praying with you, and, most of all, with God. (He knows everything about you, anyway, and is just waiting for you to be honest with Him.) Frank and Ida Mae Hammond, in **Pigs in the Parlor,** wrote "Lack of honesty keeps areas of one's life in darkness. Demon spirits thrive on darkness. . . Any sin not confessed or repented of gives the demon a 'legal right' to remain."

Perhaps your past is so painful or so embarrassing that you had rather keep it hidden deep inside instead of bringing it forth and laying it at the foot of the cross where Jesus can heal the wound.

We were praying with one young man when the Holy Spirit revealed that he had been very unhappy as a child, and that he had not been reared by his parents. When I asked him if this was true, he assured us that this was not the case. We knew immediately that for some reason he was not being open with us. God's annointing left, and the young man did not receive the release that he so desperately needed. The next day his wife called to say that he had been reared by his grandmother; his father, who was an alcoholic, had tied him to the bed on occasions and beat him severely. Satan had kept this young man in bondage with those painful childhood memories. Until a person can look honestly at his past and give it over to the Lord, he cannot be helped. It is absolutely imperative that you be honest, even though at the moment it may be very painful. Remember, you may deceive your counselor, you may deceive yourself, but you never deceive God. God is the only one who can take your hurts and heal them, but you **must** be honest with Him first.

HUMILITY

James 4:6-7 ". . . God gives strength to the humble, but sets himself against the proud and haughty. So give yourselves humbly to God. Resist the devil and he will flee from you."

James 5:16 "Admit your faults to one another and pray for each other so that you may be healed . . ."

Tied in very closely with honesty is humility. You must come humbly before the Lord. The main reason some people will not seek help is their pride. They do not want anyone to know about their background; they don't want others to realize they are in bondage because of painful memories, that they are hurting deeply inside. We are all so prone to put on a mask, and not let anyone know how we really feel. We have to strip away our hypocrisy, our deceit, our pretenses, our ego. Satan can keep us in bondage until we overcome our pride, and seek prayer and counseling.

SUMMARY

Now that you have met all the conditions, you are ready for inner healing. As I stated in the beginning, there are two main steps in inner healing:

1. Breaking Satan's bondage
2. Prayer for healing of memories

In the next chapter Ed will share with you how you can bind Satan in the name of Jesus and renounce all negative forces to reclaim your inheritance. Then you will be ready for the healing of your memories.

(**A Word of Caution**—If you feel the need of a prayer counselor to pray with you for inner healing, choose your minister or counselor carefully and under the leading of the Lord. Some people have been scarred emotionally from previous encounters with (counselors?) who heaped condemnation instead of love. Remember—by their fruit you shall know them. Choose a person who is filled with the Holy Spirit, God's love, and compassion.)

Chapter VI

Reclaiming Your Inheritance

By Ed Tapscott

Inner healing consists of two parts: reclaiming your inheritance from Satan and healing of memories. As you reclaim your inheritance you must take into consideration both your past experience and your present status as a child of God.

When you become a Christian you become a child of the Father, a joint heir with Jesus Christ of all the riches of the Father—not only of the physical riches, but even more important, of the spiritual riches. You have an **inheritance!** You have an inheritance in heaven, but you also have an inheritance here on earth. In Romans 14:17 (KJV) we read, "For the kingdom of God is not meat and drink; but righteousness, and peace, and joy in the Holy Ghost." Jesus came to bring the Kingdom of God here on earth to all who believed. This Kingdom of God is your inheritance right here on earth.

Have you ever looked at what you have as your inheritance? First, you have **Righteousness:** a right relationship with God, fellowship with God the Father. You are able to have fellowship with God every minute of every day. Jesus as the second Adam restored man to the kind of fellowship with God that man lost when the first Adam listened to the lies of Satan. This fellowship is not dependent upon what you do to earn it, but is your inheritance that you simply accept, as God's gift to you.

A second part of your inheritance is **Peace:** that calm assurance that God's in control of this world and His angels are looking out for God's children. Peace goes beyond understanding and circumstances and lets you as a child of God rise above the circumstances and lets you know, that you know, that God loves you and will see you through any problem. You, as a child of God, can simply rest in God's hands, and let Him bring into being the results.

Finally, you have **Joy** in the Holy Spirit: this is not mere happiness that results from the pleasures of the moment, but is true joy that results from your relationship with God as one of His children. You don't have to think about this joy because it simply bubbles up as you praise God. It's an effervescent kind of joy that gives a feeling of happiness and yet is based upon the sure foundation of your relationship with God. This joy wells up inside and causes you to want to praise God because of who God is—not asking for anything, but just the privilege of worshiping God.

Your inheritance from God is complete and satisfying in all things. Just as Satan came to the first of God's children, Adam and Eve, he comes to you, and uses the same techniques to rob you of your inheritance. Remember in Genesis the Bible tells how Adam and Eve had fellowship with God. Then Satan came with lies and deceit and broke off that relationship between God and Adam by appealing to Adam's desire to be like God. Satan has not changed, and still comes to you with lies and deceit to cause you to turn from God and seek your own way rather than God's way. Satan may tell you that you are not good enough to be a child of God, that you have done things too awful for God to continue to love you. Then Satan may remind you of the times you have truly failed God. Because you know that there is **some** truth in what Satan is saying, that you do not deserve to have God love you as His child, then you believe **all** that Satan says about your unworthiness. Accepting the fact that God knows all about you and me and still loves us is one of the most difficult truths of the Christian faith.

God's ways haven't changed. God works with you and me today, just the same way He has always worked with His children. God has an inheritance for you but you will have to claim your inheritance. In Genesis 12:7 God promised the land of Canaan to Abraham and his descendants. This promise was renewed to Isaac and to Jacob. The descendants of Abraham went to Egypt and after 400 years set out to return to their physical inheritance, the Land of Canaan. God had appointed Moses the leader and given him power to do mighty miracles to lead the people back to the land God had promised to Abraham. When Moses led the children of Israel back to the Jordan river and they stood ready to claim their inheritance, God had them send 12 spies over into the land to see what it was like. These spies came back with glowing reports about the beauties of the land. They said it was a land flowing with milk and honey. It was everything God had promised—but it was inhabited by the sons of Anak—a race of nine foot giants. In order to claim their inheritance, the children of Israel had to go over and defeat the nine foot giants.

God hasn't changed: that's just the way He deals with His children today. You have an inheritance of righteousness, peace, and joy in the Holy Spirit and all you have to do to claim it is to defeat the nine foot spiritual giants Satan has sent against you. Have you experienced the giant of unbelief? Have you come face to face with the giant of resentment? Have you met the giant of rejection? Or perhaps the giants of anger or hatred have come against you? Has the giant of rebellion been after you? Have you experienced the giant of depression at times? Some have to fight the giant of suicide, or the giant of unforgiveness. These giants come against you to rob you of your inheritance of the Kingdom of God.

God tells His children today the same thing he told the Children of Israel in the Old Testament. You have a beautiful inheritance from God, an inheritance that puts you in a land flowing with milk and honey. You have all you need: fellowship with God, peace, and joy in the Holy Spirit. However, you must claim this inheritance from the nine foot giants Satan has sent against you. God will be right there with you to help in this battle to defeat these giants. The fellowship of believers will be right there with you as you claim your spiritual inheritance.

Satan is so wise and knows that the important battles of life are the spiritual battles. Satan is willing to give up the temporal, physical battles of life if he can win the eternal, spiritual battle for your soul. Many church members smugly talk about how Satan is a defeated foe in their life, not realizing that he is only acting defeated because he has already won the more important spiritual battle. By allowing worry, resentment, unforgiveness, hatred, pride, rebellion, or other spiritual giants to have control of their life, they have already given Satan the important victory. Satan has deceived many Christians by not allowing them to experience God's inheritance here on this earth.

Jesus is our victory. In I Corinthians 15:57 (KJV), Paul expresses the prayer of our hearts when he says: "But thanks be to God, which giveth us the victory through our Lord Jesus Christ." Jesus is your victory over the giants Satan has sent against you. He has already defeated them on the cross and you have nothing more to fear from these giants. Victory over Satan is not something you must work to accomplish; victory is an accomplished fact, and all you must do is to claim it in the name of Jesus. In James 4:7 (KJV) you are admonished to, "Submit yourselves therefore to God. Resist the devil, and he will flee from you." You resist Satan in the name of Jesus and remind him that Jesus defeated him on the cross, and there is no further need for you to struggle with him since he is already a defeated foe. You claim your rightful inheritance and through the power of the Holy Spirit you have your inheritance.

In the Old Testament when the children of Israel crossed over the River Jordan on dry land and went on to defeat the inhabitants of the land of Canaan, they went with the assurance that God would give them victory. As long as they remained true to this assurance each victory was theirs. They marched around the walls of Jericho seven times, as God commanded, and the walls fell down. They went against each of the cities and God gave them the victory. The important thing was not the manner they used to gain each victory but the fact they were following God's command in each victory. The Children of Israel succeeded as long as they followed God's commands. But when Achan kept some gold, silver, and garments, then God allowed the next city to defeat them because they had failed to follow His commands. God deals with His children the same way today. In I Samuel 15:22 (KJV), Samuel says to Saul, ". . . to obey is better than sacrifice . . . ." Today you receive God's blessings at the point of your obedience. You claim your inheritance through obedience to the truth that God has revealed to you through His word and through the Holy Spirit.

To claim the inheritance you have in Jesus, you must take authority over the giants Satan has sent against you. Renounce each of these giants in the name of Jesus, and command each spiritual giant to leave you and have no influence in your life again. As Christians we have set a hierarchy of sins with some sins worse than others. God views all sin as singular and as rebellion against Him. There is no spiritual force Satan can send against you that you cannot have authority over in the name of Jesus.

Ask the Holy Spirit to reveal to you the things that Satan has sent against you and then as He reveals them, renounce each one and command that force or spirit to leave you in the name of Jesus. For example, if the Holy Spirit reveals that you have been tormented by a spirit of rejection, you simply say: "Spirit of rejection, out in the name of Jesus." If possible, pray with someone who can lift you up in prayer as you renounce the involvement with Satan and take authority over the giants Satan has sent against you. Some of the giants Satan sends against people are:

pride	doubt
unbelief	condemnation
rebellion	rejection
loneliness	anger
hatred	resentment
bitterness	suicide
anxiety	unforgiveness
paranoia	intellectualism
lying	indecision
procrastination	self-pity
temper	self-will
criticism	insecurity
inferiority	timidity
jealousy	fantasy
indifference	depression
defeat	hopelessness
worry	fear
tension	fear of disapproval

nervousness	schizophrenia
suspicion	confusion
frustration	self-deception
fear of failure	deceit
covetousness	greed
intolerance	grief
sorrow	death
gluttony	lust
adultery	cults
occult	false religions
alcohol	nicotine
drugs	competition
fatigue	infirmity
spiritism	guilt

Go back through the list above and in each instance ask the Holy Spirit to reveal to you if that is a negative force or a giant or a spirit that Satan has used to help defeat you. For each of the negative forces the Holy Spirit reveals to you as one that is coming against you, repeat this authority statement over that negative spirit: "Spirit of _____, out in the name of Jesus."

God has provided you the power to rebuke Satan and take authority over him. As you exercise that power, the Lord gives you new power and authority and provides all that is necessary for you to have complete victory.

Now through the power of the Holy Spirit ask Jesus to put into your heart and mind the rightful inheritance God has promised you. Ask Jesus to give you the spirit of joy, the spirit of peace, the comfort that comes from a right relationship with God. Ask Jesus to fill you with LOVE. Not love as defined by this world's standards, but love like Jesus knew. A love that is supernatural and that extends to all relationships in your life. Ask Jesus to fill every void in your life with all the fruit of the Spirit, with all the positive forces—ask Jesus to fill you completely with the Holy Spirit.

Remember, just binding Satan and renouncing all the negative forces is not enough. You must constantly keep your spiritual house clean and filled where these negative forces cannot return. (See Luke 11:24-26, Matt. 12:43-45) Ask Jesus to constantly fill you with the Holy Spirit and all the fruit of the Spirit.

A word of caution, don't look for an evil spirit in every person as an explanation for every wrong thing they do. Some people enjoy blaming Satan for their misbehavior when the person actually needs to practice will power and self control. Also, remember Christians can not be **possessed,** but they can be **oppressed** by Satan. Don't let Satan frighten you, and don't give him more credit than he deserves.

The next step in inner healing is prayer for the healing of memories—If you had a spirit of fear, the Lord not only wants to set you free from that oppression, but He also wants to heal the memory of the incident when the fear entered.

Chapter VII

Healing of Memories

The following is a prayer for healing of memories. When you read this prayer, for the most effective results go to a place that is quiet so you can be alone and really commune with the Lord. Seek the Lord humbly and honestly with praise and thanksgiving. Remember—you must ask Him first to forgive all your sins. Make sure you have asked Jesus into your heart as your personal Savior. As a believer, take the authority the Lord has given you and renounce all the negative forces Satan has sent against you. Ask the Holy Spirit to reveal these forces to you. After you have renounced all negative forces, ask Jesus to fill the void with His love, His joy, His peace. Now, visualize Jesus walking hand-in-hand with you back through every second of your life. As the Holy Spirit brings to your mind memories of unpleasant situations, take Jesus into that episode with you. He is all love, light and peace and can redeem those unpleasant memories. In the same way He forgives sins of long ago, He can heal painful memories from your past. Ask Him to give you the measure of faith needed to believe that you will be set free and your memories will be healed. Thank Him in advance for the miracle He is going to work in your life.

PRAYER FOR HEALING OF MEMORIES
(Make This Your OWN Personal Prayer)

Father, I thank you for your Son Jesus who died on the cross not only for my sins, but for my hurts and for my fears. I thank you that Jesus is the same yesterday, today and forever, and that He wants me to be completely whole: mind, soul, body and spirit. Lord Jesus, I ask you to walk back through every second of my life, to heal me and to make me whole. Go back into the third and fourth generation and break all harmful genetic ties.

Jesus, you knew all about me even before I was born. Thank

you for being there as life began. If fear or any other negative force was transmitted to me as I was in my mother's womb, set me free from those things. Thank you, Lord Jesus, for being there when I was born, and for loving me. (Some came into this world not being loved and not being wanted, and they felt such rejection. Oh, Lord Jesus, from the very beginning fill each one with your precious love.)

Lord, walk back through every second of my life during those early years. (Some were separated from parents because of sickness or death, some were born into families where they did not receive the love that was needed.) Lord Jesus, please go back and fill every void; give the love that was not received. Remove every hurt, every feeling of rejection. Take away all fears: fears of darkness, fears of falling, fears of animals, fears of being lost. I thank you Jesus for setting me free and for healing me.

I pray Lord that you will take my hand, go back in time and walk to school with me. At times I felt so shy, so afraid to leave home and go into new situations. Jesus there were times I felt embarrassment or failure at school, will you take away those memories? When I was treated harshly by a teacher or I was hurt by classmates, please heal those hurts. Some fears entered during those first school years, fear of speaking in public, or fear of failure. Thank you for healing those hurts and for setting me free from those fears. I thank you and I praise you.

Lord Jesus, I thank you for my mother. (For those who did not have the love of a mother, please fill that void, that empty place and give them the love that was needed.) I ask you to stand between my mother and me and let your divine love flow between us. I ask forgiveness from my mother for any way I have hurt her or failed her and I forgive her for any way she hurt or failed me.

Lord Jesus, I thank you for my dad. (For those who did not feel the love of an earthly dad, please give them all the love they needed but didn't receive.) Stand between my dad and me. I pray that your divine love will mend any broken relationship. I ask forgiveness from my dad for any way I hurt or failed him, and I forgive him for any way he hurt or failed me.

I lift up my brothers and sisters to you. Where there were

feelings of competition, jealousy, or resentment, I ask that your healing power and love mend every broken relationship. I forgive each brother and sister for hurting or failing me and I ask their forgiveness for the ways I hurt or failed them.

Thank you, Lord, for being there in my teenage years and when I was in Junior High and High School. There were new emotions and new fears. As each painful memory is brought to my mind, I pray that you will take a spiritual eraser and just wipe the pain from my mind and heal me. During those times that I tried things that were dangerous, I thank you for being there with your protective hand. Take away any feeling of humiliation, embarrassment, guilt, fear or failure. (Some were teased because of race, appearance, size, or poverty and were wounded so deeply.) Let me know that you loved me and that you were there in every situation. (For those young people who experimented with drugs, that left their minds confused, Lord Jesus we pray you will repair the damage. Let them think clearly again; let them receive your healing. Let each one know you love them and that you can redeem the past.)

As each of us started to leave home, there were new fears, frustrations, or hurts. (Some wanted to go on to college and were not able to; others were not able to enter the profession they dreamed of and they felt such disappointment.) Jesus, heal every disappointment and every hurt.

Thank you for being there as we entered marriage. (For some it was such a beautiful new beginning. For others it was a nightmare.) Jesus, please take away every hurt. I pray that you will stand in between me and my mate and heal every hurt. I am saying to my mate, I forgive you for hurting me and I ask your forgiveness for hurting you. Lord Jesus, through Your divine love, I thank you for mending every broken relationship, and wiping away every painful memory. (Where there has been the heartbreak of divorce and there are feelings of guilt, rejection, bitterness and loneliness, take away all those negative feelings. Heal the deep wounds and erase the painful memories. Jesus, fill each mate with forgiveness, Your divine love and healing power.)

Thank you, Lord, for my children. Take away any feeling I have of failure or guilt as a parent. When I punished unwisely or was too possessive with my love, when words were spoken in criticism or anger, I pray you will heal any hurt that was caused. I ask their forgiveness and I forgive them for hurting me.

Lord, I thank you for being there during those terrifying times of accidents, those times of sickness or surgery. I ask you now to take away the horror, the fear and the memory of the pain. Set me free from the trauma I felt. Thank you for being there during times of sorrow. I thank you for taking my hand and walking through the valley with me; I thank you for lifting the burden; I thank you for taking away my sorrow, my grief, and my mourning. I thank you for giving me your joy and your peace.

Now, Lord Jesus, thank you for walking back through every second of my life up to this exact moment. Thank you for healing me of all my hurts, my fears, my painful memories, and my guilt; for setting me free. Thank you for filling me with your love. Help me to love myself. Help me to love others. But most of all, Jesus, help me to love you as I should. I thank you for giving me joy. I thank you for giving me peace. Thank you, Jesus! I thank you for going way down deep into the darkest recesses of my mind and cleansing me. I thank you for healing my mind, my emotions, and my memories. I thank you, Jesus, for making me whole; and I give you all the praise and all the glory. Amen.

(When my friend, Bette Jo, read this manuscript she said, "You don't have a prayer for the elderly and one is really needed." I felt as if it were the Lord speaking through her. My spirit really bore witness with her comment. The following is the prayer the Lord gave.)

A Special Prayer for the Elderly

Lord Jesus, I pray that you will bless in a special way those who have reached the golden years. As they look back over their long life, please heal all their hurts, take away all painful memories, take away any feelings of regret, remorse, bitterness or disappointment.

Lord, set them free from any fear of dying. There is such a feeling of loneliness and rejection for some; let them know how much you love them. Please put your arms around them so that they feel your presence; be so close, so very real to them.

Lord, may they reach out to others with more love and forgiveness. Mend any broken relationships they may have.

Reveal the mysteries of heaven to them Lord, let them know you are waiting right there to bring them home. Home, where they will be free from pain, disease, where they will be free from financial worry, from problems. Home, where they can talk with you, can talk with the disciples, home where they will be reunited with loved ones.

Thank you, Lord, for touching them by Your Spirit, for renewing their minds, for refreshing their memories with the precious, pleasant, and wonderful events that occurred back through the years. Let them know how deeply you love them.

Thank you Jesus! Amen.

Chapter VIII

How to Keep Your Inner Healing

Suppose you have been prayed for, and the Lord has done a tremendous and beautiful inner healing. You feel like a different person; every fiber of your being is filled with peace, joy and love. You are completely set free from any bondage and all painful memories are totally healed . . . but . . . if you invite those negative attitudes and confessions back, if you deliberately start dwelling on the old wounds, they will certainly give you trouble again.

Think of it this way: Haven't you seen a child with a skinned knee? It is healing beautifully, but then he starts rubbing and scratching the scab, and before long the wound is an open sore again. We must forget the past and look to the future. We must not reopen healing wounds.

I want to share some things with you that will help you keep your inner healing.

1. Pray without ceasing.

   Live in an attitude of prayer. Wake up with a prayer and go to sleep with a prayer on your lips. Pray about all things . . . big and small. Pray when you are driving the car, before you answer the phone, as you're shopping, etc. Pray in the spirit without ceasing.

2. Read your Bible regularly.

   Just as you must have physical food to survive physically, you must have spiritual food to survive spiritually. You get that spiritual food from reading God's Word. Read your Bible every day.

3. Praise the Lord always.

   Develop a positive outlook. In 1 Thessalonians 5:16-18

the Bible says, "Always be joyful. Always keep on praying. No matter what happens, always be thankful, for this is God's will for you who belong to Christ Jesus." So, praise God **in all** circumstances. Do not give way to negative confessions. **Praise** God for your hurts, **praise** Him for your painful memories and **praise** Him for your problems! "Aways give thanks **for** everything . . . ." (Eph. 5:20).

I woke up one morning with some problems really bothering me, depression was creeping in. I could have sat on the sofa all day and moped, but I literally walked through the house forcing myself to praise the Lord. With determination I jumped from the sofa and walked to the living room window, "Thank you Lord for the trees, the flowers. Thank you Lord that I can see; thank you Lord for my eyes." As I walked into the den I could hear the birds in the trees off the patio, "Thank you Lord for the birds; thank you Lord that I can hear; thank you for my ears." I walked into the kitchen and stooped to pick something off the floor, "Thank you Lord that I can walk and bend; thank you for my legs and for my feet." With increasing lightness and joy my hands shot up into the air and then I clapped them. "Why, thank you Lord for my hands and thank you that I can move them." I quickly thought of all the many things I had to be thankful for— loving parents, my family, my husband, our children and home. "Oh, Lord you are so good!" By this time, my depression began to lift, and I was able to thank Him for the problems. This only took about ten minutes, but by that time, my inner spirit was soaring, and the problems didn't seem so big.

4. Daily commit yourself to the Lord.

Daily ask for His guidance and wisdom. Give up all practices that do not glorify the Lord. Ask the Holy Spirit to reveal to you the things you are doing that are not pleasing to the Lord, and then . . . stop doing them! Don't say you **can't** stop some habit. The Bible says, we **can** do all things through Christ who strengthens us. (See Phil. 4:13 KJV) Each morning say, Lord, I commit this day to you—every thought, word, and deed. Pray daily to be filled with the fruit of the spirit: love, joy, peace, patience, kindness, goodness, faithfulness, gentleness and self-control. (Galatians 5:22-23)

5. Dedicate your home to the Lord.

Surround yourself with spiritual things that glorify the Lord. Listen to Christian music, read Christian books, subscribe to Christian magazines, listen to spirit-filled tapes. (We never go on a long trip without a tape recorder and cassettes by spirit-filled musicians and teachers. We listen until we reach our destination.) Throw away all books, magazines, pictures, articles, and music that do not glorify the Lord. Choose television programs carefully, not only for your children but for yourself. Ask yourself, if Jesus walked into this room would I have this particular show on? Also, be very careful which movies you allow your children to see or the ones you see. I realize there must be a balance in our lives. Someone has said we can become so "heavenly minded" we are no "earthly" good. I'm just saying we must put the Lord **first** in every area of our life. Pray for a perfect balance of being in the world but not of the world. Jesus does not honor compromise.

6. Stand firm against Satan.

Take authority over Satan when he comes against you, and bind him in the name of Jesus. (See Matt. 12:29) If a spirit of fear is bothering you, say, "You spirit of fear, I cast you out in the name of Jesus." (See Mark 16:17) Remember, "Resist the devil and he will flee from you." (James 4:7) Keep repeating over and over, perfect love casts out all fear. We need to keep our eyes on Jesus and not on Satan. But God warns us to "Be careful—watch out for attacks from Satan, your great enemy. He prowls around like a hungry, roaring lion, looking for some victim to tear apart. Stand firm when he attacks. . . ." (1 Pet. 5:8-9)

7. Get into a Spirit-filled fellowship.

If your church does not teach that Jesus Christ died for your sins, find a church that does. Ask the Holy Spirit to lead you to a prayer group where you can feel the power of the Holy Spirit and the moving of the Holy Spirit. Make the effort to go hear Christian speakers and take your family with you.

8. Have a prayer partner.

You need a prayer partner, one with whom you can share your burdens and praises. The Bible says ". . . if two of you agree down here on earth concerning anything you ask for, my Father in heaven will do it for you." (Matthew 18:19) If you feel Satan coming against you, and if after you pray the oppression still doesn't leave, then ask your prayer partner to pray with you immediately. Remember prayer partners—"do not share these requests with anyone else but the Lord!!!"

9. Accept God's Inner Healing.

Accept the inner healing that God gives you. Accept it by faith. You may say, "I don't have enough faith." The Bible says we only need to have faith as big as a grain of mustard seed. (See Matthew 17:20) If you don't have even that much faith then have faith in the faith of Jesus. Don't look at the evidence or the circumstances but stand on God's promises. The Bible says life or death is in your mouth. Only let positive confessions come from your mouth.

10. Constantly forgive and restore.

The moment someone hurts you, give it to the Lord immediately. Not that night, not the next day, but right then. The moment you hurt someone say, "I'm sorry, forgive me," and ask God's forgiveness. Go into the "construction" business, constructing bridges between broken relationships. If you have offended someone openly, ask their forgiveness. But if they are not aware of your inner feelings, be silent. Ask God's forgiveness for your ugly attitude. Don't go charging up to someone with piety and say, "I've always thought you were terrible, I really couldn't tolerate you, but now I'm sorry, will you forgive me?" Obviously that would do more harm than good. If you each know there have been harsh words, dishonesty, gossip, or false accusations, go to that person and ask their forgiveness. Don't stop there! If you have spread false rumors, try to repair the damage you have caused. Try to restore and rebuild every broken relationship. Share God's love and His peace continually with others.

Retaining your inner healing may not be easy, but remember you are the only one who can keep the inner healing God provided for you. God will do His part, but you have to do your part!

Certainly, you may have valleys, disappointments and failures. We all do, life is a constant climb up the ladder toward God. We may climb up three rungs of the ladder and slip down one. We may climb up five and slip back four. But we **can be overcomers** by resting in the Lord, by submitting to Him, obeying Him, by leaning on Him, by trusting Him.

Imagine yourself in a boat with Jesus as the captain. The seas may be very rough and treacherous, the wind blowing with a mighty gale, the rain falling in torrents, the lightning striking all around you. But, with Jesus as your captain, He will calm that storm, He will guide your ship safely home, He will keep you in the hollow of His hand.

We Can Be Victorious!

We Can Be OVERCOMERS!

Chapter IX

He Touched Them

One of our most cherished honors is to be asked to pray for a child of a friend. It is beautiful and humbling when someone trusts you enough to place their most prized possession in your hands; when they have enough faith in your relationship with the Lord to ask you to counsel and pray with that child. We were very honored by this responsibility recently.

My friend was called to her son's school for a conference. The teacher explained that there were some "warning signals" concerning their eight-year-old son's behavior. Here are a few of the reasons the teacher gave for her concern:

1. frequent daydreaming
2. no desire to play with other boys
3. preoccupation with fantasy
4. poor grades even though he had a very high I.Q.
5. obsession with wearing white pants, white shirt, and white sweater every day (while this is not serious, neither is it typical of eight-year-old boys)

She suggested the parents take him to a psychiatrist before more serious problems developed.

My husband, Ed, has a Ph.D. degree and has been the Dean of a College of Behavioral Sciences, I have a Master's degree in this related field, but this was not the reason we were asked to counsel and pray with this young boy. We were asked because with all our hearts we believe Jesus Christ can change negative traits and habits, renew minds and channel God-given talents in a positive way.

The father, mother, and eight-year-old came to our home one evening for prayer. The boy, a winsome, handsome young man, was very intelligent and endearing.

Ed and I had him sit between us on the sofa. His parents seated themselves across from us. At first Ed and I spoke softly with him concerning school, his likes and dislikes, any fears he had, the things that caused him problems. Later we talked with him about Jesus and asked him when he had invited Christ into his heart as his Savior. Then, gently and simply, we explained that Satan sometimes sends fears against us; that he makes us interested in things that really don't glorify Jesus.

Then, we knelt by the sofa and very, very quietly and gently (but with the authority given us by Jesus), bound Satan from this precious boy's life. We asked Jesus to break all the negative forces Satan had sent against him. One spirit Satan had sent against him was a spirit of loneliness. Now remember, he was one of four boys, and he had not shared the fact that he was very lonely, but the Holy Spirit revealed it to us as one of the main binding spirits. On the way home that night he told his mother, "Mother, the **Lord** had to tell her how lonely I was, because I never told anyone." Also, there was a spirit of fantasy (which we believe entered from some of the television shows he had seen).

After all the negative forces had been bound from his life, we asked Jesus to fill him with positive forces—the love of Jesus, inner peace, confidence, the ability to relate to others in the way he wanted to, etc. Then, we prayed for the healing of his memories, for healing from any fears or hurts he had.

Later the parents showed us the school notebook their son used before prayer for his inner healing. Grades and notes from the teacher were: "He needs to be more responsible." "Grades unsatisfactory—He can do better." "Grades—poor," etc. Two days after his inner healing his teacher placed on his spelling paper, "He is improving in school." And to the young boy, the teacher wrote, "I am so proud of your improvement. **Everyone** has noticed the **new you.**" Six days later, the teacher wrote, "He has had a great week in school. Things are looking up. Grade— terrific!" Two weeks later, a note to the young boy from his teacher read, "I am so proud of you—you are improving **so** much **so** fast!"

Weeks after prayer, the mother said that so many of his habits had changed. He enjoyed playing with the other boys. Now he preferred to wear blue jeans and a levi jacket—normal attire for an eight-year-old boy. Satan was defeated before he had a chance to damage this precious, young life. We are strongly convinced that the Lord has His hand on this boy, or Satan wouldn't have tried so hard to ensnare him into a fantasy world. (We praise you, Jesus, for all that You did for this young boy.)

The Lord uses different avenues and ways to channel His love and healing power: telephones, television, cassette tapes, books. I'm so thankful and I praise Him that He is not limited by time or space. A friend telephoned one day to say she had been told by her doctor that tests showed there was 99 percent chance she had cancer. She was scheduled for immediate surgery. Her mother had died of cancer with identical symptoms only three years before so there was deep concern even though they were relying on the Lord. Many, many prayers were being offered up to the Lord concerning this lovely Christian.

The day before she went to the hospital we prayed over the telephone (miles apart) for the healing of the painful memories concerning her mother's death. Now she was ready to face surgery free from fear. The next morning when the doctor operated he found no trace of cancer. God had answered the many prayers sent heavenward by a host of friends.

A few days later we again had prayer over the telephone for some other painful memories. The power of the Lord literally "crackled" over the telephone lines as we agreed in prayer— waves upon waves of His precious Holy Spirit rolled over us. A few weeks later she shared that the Lord had completely healed the deep hurts in her life and had completely wiped away the painful memories. Several months later she said, "You know my surgery was worth it just to have prayer for the healing of all those painful memories and to have Jesus heal me of them.

My husband and I witnessed the complete transformation of a young couple who had been deeply hurt by a pastor who forced them to confess a sin before the entire congregation. As this was shared I kept thinking about Jesus' comment to the woman who was brought to Him, "Let him without sin cast the first stone." There had been misdeeds, but they had been confessed, and the Lord had forgiven. It was just some members of the church who would not let this couple forget their past.

The Lord directed as I prayed with her for healing of memories that she visualize Jesus standing with her as she had to confess her sin before the church—then to visualize Jesus walking down the aisle with her at her wedding. This act of having Jesus share the experience with her brought healing. This young couple now is part of a fellowship which shows love and forgiveness. They are maturing in the Lord, constantly witnessing for Him and ministering to others. Our hearts overflow with love as we watch the Lord work through them.

A young woman with deep guilt feelings, who was on the verge of divorce and literally hated herself, wrote these comments after we prayed with her:

> I have not been the same person since prayer for inner healing and healing of memories. Jesus did a complete work that day. I am free and my past no longer hurts me. My mind has truly been renewed. All my friends see the difference, but most important, my husband sees and knows he has a new wife. He really loves this one . . . I can't begin to tell you everything that has happened or changed but I have not had even a touch of asthma, nor allergic reaction to cats. P.T.L. The real me on the inside is so different. I'm more serious. I'm not a phony . . . My life has purpose now. I am not struggling . . . there is such **peace.** I see the whole world through brand new eyes. Jesus is so beautiful . . . I am free. I feel like I've been born again. **I AM ALIVE.** Praise Jesus!!!!

The change in this woman was a miracle. When I first met her, she arrived wearing a black, leather-like jacket, men's jeans, cowboy boots. Her hair was cut in a boyish style. She shared her story of how she had been associated with lesbians when she was in the service. She had since married, but her marriage was crumbling. In fact she was taking a three month bus trip across the United States, then planned to go back and file divorce proceedings. The Lord just "happened" to have her stop over in Houston and she just "happened" to end up in our home for inner healing. Of course it didn't "just happen." There are no "co"incidences in the Lord—just "God" incidences.

As we were praying for her to be set free from all the guilt and bondage, the Holy Spirit revealed a strong spirit of self-hate. When she tried to say, "You spirit of self-hate, I renounce you in the name of Jesus," she literally could not get the words out of her mouth. Her face turned red, she grabbed at her throat. She kept struggling to say, "Self-hate, out in the name of Jesus." I quickly said, "Satan, you are bound in the name of Jesus, you have absolutely no control over this woman, we plead the blood of Jesus over her, you must loose your grip on her immediately." Of course it is not our power at all, it is the power of God, but Satan instantly loosed his grip. She said, "You know it felt as if someone was on the inside of me saying, 'I will not come out, I will not come out, this is my home, I will not leave.'" We finished ministering inner healing; she left our city and continued her trip over the country. The Lord was doing a mighty work in her and by the time she arrived back home, she wanted her marriage to work, she wanted to change and be the type of wife and homemaker she should be. We have received several letters from her and she is still rejoicing and serving the Lord.

A young divorcee related that when she was two years old, her mother suffered a nervous breakdown. She could remember wanting her mother to play with her, to hold her, but her mother was in bed sick and could not. Because this little child felt such rejection, she started sucking her thumb for comfort. When her dad tried to make her stop sucking her thumb, she started stuttering. As she grew older, naturally, she stopped sucking her thumb, but she could remember the embarrassment that came from her stuttering. Even when she was in her teenage years if she talked too fast she would stumble over her words, and someone would say, "Now just slow down, start over again and speak more slowly." She felt more rejection when her marriage ended in divorce.

She outgrew the thumb sucking, the stuttering, but the deep rooted feeling of rejection took another form—smoking. So, when she was lonely, felt insecure or rejected—she reached not for her thumb, but a cigarette. She had tried many times to stop smoking but was unable to do so. We asked Jesus to fill the void and give her all the love she needed as a child but didn't receive. After Jesus healed all her painful memories she found the need for cigarettes was completely gone. She telephoned after prayer for inner healing to say, "I'm filled with an inner calm, assurance, and peace that I've never had before. I haven't had a cigarette in several weeks, and all the desire to smoke is gone. I have a love for Jesus that I've never had before!" PTL.

When the Lord touched a pharmacy student from Purdue she wrote:

> After prayer with you for inner healing God took away all the tension in my stomach, my fingers, my legs, and even my eyes . . . I could feel the peace of Jesus inside after prayer. I slept super well that night, no tossing and turning, and I have since, except when the Lord wanted me to pray and He **had** me to wake up . . .
>
> I use to eat almost everything in sight. Well, I haven't eaten between meals and don't feel hungry. I've lost sixteen pounds, just because He took away all nervous tension. There seems to be a glow all over I've never had before. Best of all I have real peace on the inside. Inner healing has made me free to get to know Jesus better. P.S. He even healed my eyes and I can see colors now—P.T.L.!

(This girl had 20/80-20/100 vision. A few weeks after prayer she returned to her ophthalmologist. He immediately asked her why she was not wearing her glasses. "The Lord has healed my eyes, but I want medical verification," she explained. After a thorough examination the doctor found her eyesight to be 20/20.)

After we prayed the prayer for healing of memories over television, a man from another state wrote:

> I've long had trouble effecting a personal witness because of shyness which I did not understand. I still do not know what caused this shyness, but as I prayed with you I felt Jesus touching me. I am happy to report that this hampering force in my Christian witness has been removed. Praise God!

During this same television show the Lord gave me word of knowledge that someone had dropped a cafeteria tray and suffered embarrassment from this minor incident. The next morning at 8:00 sharp a lady called to say she had been watching the show; she had suffered that embarrassment, and that the Lord had healed the memory. She was from a small company town where everyone knew her. The first Sunday she was away from home at college she was so lonely, frightened, homesick. Even being in God's house that morning didn't take away her homesickness. She entered the college cafeteria after church, empty, but not hungry. After she filled her tray and started walking to the table she slipped. She shared later:

My tray clanged and clattered across the terrazzo floor like a fire gong and particles of food flew through the air like confetti. Almost as soon as I had fallen, many of my fellow students rushed to my aid, helping me to my feet, picking up the tray, dishes, and food. They pretended not to notice the milk dripping from my dress or the tears welling up in my eyes, and they insisted that I go through the serving line again. I wanted to run and hide but did go back through the line; I only nibbled at the food on my plate. Twenty years later, my Jesus ministered to me via a TV program to let me know that He was with me the day I fell and He was with me as I watched the TV program. I felt the touch of His healing love as He erased the humiliation of the moment from my memory.

A spirit-filled television producer, we will call John, related his experience of how the Lord anointed a cassette tape. He and his lovely wife were sharing Jesus with a friend who had deep psychological and emotional problems. The man was addicted to prescribed drugs, had been unemployed for ten months, and was having severe family problems. One night at eleven o'clock John and his wife went to the man's house, and had him listen to our tape on inner healing. The Lord ministered to him as he was listening and when the tape was finished John and his wife prayed with him. The man was touched by God's power and was instantly transformed. He was delivered, cleansed, and healed. Not only did God set him free from drugs, but he soon found a job and his family problems were solved. Today that man is witnessing for the Lord and singing in his church choir.

As I said before, the Lord uses all means and avenues to channel His healing and cleansing power. He uses the telephone, television shows, cassette tapes, books, individuals. It is not the person nor the instrument that heals . . . it is only **God's anointing power** and that alone!

Our joy has known no bounds as we have witnessed the transformation of lives of couples who come into our living room so angry with each other they were ready for divorce. Resentment, deep hurts, jealousy, suspicion, all the negative emotions were there, but after prayer for inner healing the Lord performed His beautiful healing process and we shared their happiness as they left arm in arm. It is watching Ephesians

2:15 come alive . . . "Then he took the two groups that had been opposed to each other and made them parts of himself; thus he fused us together to become one new person, and at last there was peace."

God has privileged us to see young people who have been on drugs, fearful of life, feeling so inadequate to face life, shoulders sagging, feet dragging, suddenly square their shoulders, find new courage and self acceptance. It is wonderful to see these young people with a glow on their faces as if a light has been turned on. (Thank you Lord for your miracle of **transformation**).

God's redeeming power has made us so thankful. It has made us bow down before the Lord and praise Him for manifesting Himself in such beautiful ways. The Word says in Malachi 4:6 "His preaching will bring fathers and children together again, to be of one mind and heart. . . ." Many young people after prayer for inner healing say, "The first thing I must do is ask my parents' forgiveness," or "I'm going to start praying for my family so they will come to know the Lord." God is still bringing together fathers and children, mothers and children, husbands and wives. (Thank you Lord for your miracle of **reconciliation.**)

A stepmother who had gone through life feeling unloved, miserable, dejected, oppressed, who was filled with resentment and self-pity was changed over night through inner healing. She immediately started rebuilding the bridges of reconciliation between herself and members of her family. After Jesus touched her, a beautiful radiance was on her face, love flowed from her heart, praises to the Lord became second nature to her—even when things went wrong. She wrote:

> Ever dumped over a cereal bowl full of milk in the refrigerator—and watched it run down the sides—both inside and out? And this formerly uptight, striking-out, type of person—watched the milk trickle down for a moment—said, 'Well—thank you Lord'—and then giggled the whole time I was washing it all up—Just another reminder from our Lord that He has touched me. Praise His Holy Name!

Recently a church acquaintance asked this previously critical and negative person what had happened to her. She said, "I know the Lord has healed you! You're so different, there is something new and beautiful about you." P.T.L.!

Some individuals have come with minor problems, others have come with deep, excruciating, emotional wounds, and desperately needed God's healing balm poured over their wounds. Some people were healed immediately—for others, the battle to reclaim their inheritance was long and tedious.

I'm reminded of the story of a person who fought such a battle for total inner healing over a period of many months. But the greater the battle—the greater the victory.

Over a period of one year's time we witnessed this person fall from the plateau of success and money achieved by deception, to the level of such despair that he was on the verge of suicide. After his double life was discovered and his world crumbled, we watched him climb out of this black abyss and back up the ladder to God, to peace, to respectability.

He struggled every inch of the way. There were times when he literally hung on by one tiny thread, his faith gone. We could only say, "Let others have the faith for you; remember God promised He would not send more than you can bear. He promised He would not leave nor forsake you."

This story began one night at twelve o'clock as we were driving home from a meeting. The Holy Spirit brought a person's name to my mind and this warning, "Jerry* is on the verge of suicide." As soon as we arrived home I called a mutual friend who had Jerry's unlisted telephone number in another city. I shared with them what the Holy Spirit had revealed. They called Jerry. He was indeed at that very moment contemplating suicide. Desperation, depression, futility, fear, embarrassment, and guilt had completely overwhelmed him. Just that week he had been discovered living a double life— living a lie.

The next day he came for prayer for inner healing. Here was a person filled with pride and ego who gave the impression of being everything he was not. But on the inside there was the broken heart of an unwanted child. A child beaten physically and verbally, scorned, ridiculed, despised and unloved. Every

*The name has been changed.

79

move he made while growing up was met by disappointment and failure. Death took the only person who really cared and loved him. Jerry made a vow to himself: "I will succeed, I will, no matter what, I will become somebody." There were years of heartache, a broken marriage, sickness, lack of money, despair, and bitterness.

His determination to become "somebody" was channeled into the wrong direction. Through a series of innocent looking episodes, a tangled web of deceit was started. The net grew and grew and became stronger until there was a time he almost believed the deception himself. As is always true of deception, he kept sinking deeper and deeper. For years he lived a double life. One of financial success on one hand, and on the other hand a life of crime and deceit. Always driving with one eye glancing over his shoulder—constantly changing his address, changing his automobiles, changing telephone numbers, and even appearance. Always the fear of being found out—but yet not being afraid of anyone or anything. There were years of covering over inner turmoil with sarcasm and hositilty, hurt someone before they hurt you; put up a front before someone finds out the real you.

We prayed with him to be set free from the bondage of rejection, deceit, pride, ego, resentment, hatred, bitterness, suicide, murder, anger, depression, guilt, unforgiveness, etc. The Holy Spirit revealed and ministered and set him free. Jesus healed the excruciatingly painful memories. But Jerry's battle the next several months was a constant struggle. He literally went through a trial by fire. There were times when the spirit of deceit would come back so strongly it almost overwhelmed him. There was a time when pride and exaggeration seemed to be completely taking control again. Events occurred that left him completely at God's mercy—his back was against the wall. Hours were spent pouring over God's Word and reading what the Bible said about lying, pride, and haughtiness. There were many times of saying, "God will do what He says, but you must do your part too."

When things got to the point where he literally could go no place but up, when all pride was finally gone and he stood broken before the Lord—God's hand began to move. The pieces of God's puzzle started falling into place. Finally, after many months, Jerry's inner healing was completed. He reclaimed his inheritance of righteousness, peace, and joy. Victory in Jesus was his!!!!!

Spiritual warfare is not easy! God's cleansing is sometimes very painful! But oh! how precious the sweet, sweet fragrance of God's victory when the battle is won!

In this chapter we have shared just some of the testimonies of how God has touched and healed and made whole through inner healing. Again, let me state we had absolutely nothing to do with it. If the Lord had not set free and healed, it would not have been done.

The Lord does not love these people more than you. He knows all about you. He loves you as a very special, unique individual. If you had been the only person on this earth, Jesus would have died on the Cross **just for you.**

Do you have a deep hurt? Do you have a broken relationship? Is your heart breaking? Is your mind confused with fear and torment? Have you suffered severe disappointment or failure? Have you lost a loved one, and are you crying out in loneliness and despair? Are you loaded down with guilt and condemnation? Do you feel the Lord could never forgive you? Do you feel so unloved, unworthy and useless?

Tell God your problems, tell Him you're hurting—Ask Him to forgive you and to heal you. He wants to set you free. He wants to cleanse you. He wants to heal every area of your life—Spirit, Soul, Body.

JUST ASK HIM!

This is my closing prayer for you—

> May the God of **peace** himself make you entirely pure and devoted to God; and may your **spirit** and **soul,** and **body** be kept strong and blameless until that day when our Lord Jesus Christ comes back again. (1 Thessalonians 5:23)

In the name of Jesus we pray—

Amen.

Appendix A

Ministering Inner Healing

Of all the many types of ministries, there is no greater need to show love, compassion, gentleness, discretion, and patience than when praying for inner healing and for the healing of memories. God may send a person with a broken heart, a wounded spirit, a confused mind, a shattered personality, or one bowed by Satan's bondage. In all ministries, one must rely completely on God, but it is absolutely mandatory in the ministry of inner healing. It is a ministry in which the Holy Spirit has to minister through discernment, word of knowledge, wisdom. The Holy Spirit alone can reveal the real source or the root of a problem.

Your responsibility as a counselor is to show people love— God's love, your love, and to take them to the Lord in prayer believing with them in faith that the Lord wants to make them WHOLE. They may not have faith—so you will need to have enough faith for them.

Prayer for inner healing requires time. Allow enough time. Never attempt deep inner healing unless you have at least an hour — usually, allow two hours without interruptions. Remember, when individuals come they probably are very nervous, a little frightened, perhaps a bit reluctant to share their problems. So, first of all, make them feel welcome and try to put them at ease. Show them that you are interested, concerned, and that you really do care about them. Be sincere. Assure them that the details shared with you will not be passed on to anyone else.

It is not always possible to have a prayer warrior present with you as you minister, and most people request they be able to come by themselves. Many of the things that are shared are so personal and the hurts so deep, that they do not want anyone else present. It is vital, though, to have people lifting you up in prayer as you minister.

A word of caution—It is better not to pray with anyone of the opposite sex alone.

We start the prayer and counseling session with a prayer similiar to this:

> Heavenly Father we commit this time to You. We confess with our mouth that we will accept no thought, word or impression that does not come from You. We ask forgiveness for our own sins whereby we might be clean vessels. Thank you Lord for Your power and Your protection. Thank you that we can be overcomers because of the shed blood of Jesus. Lord, just send Your guardian and ministering angels and station them all around. Thank you for Your promise that, He that is in me is greater than he that is in the world*. In the name of Jesus we pray. Amen.

The counseling time is usually divided into four parts:

1. Listening as the person shares his problems. (Remember, you do the listening; they do the talking. As you are listening to them, you are also listening to the Holy Spirit as He reveals the source of the problem to you.)

2. Praying to break Satan's bondage. (Reclaiming their inheritance) Remember, this prayer can be done quietly and gently, but it must be done with the authority of Jesus.

3. Praying for healing of memories. Asking Jesus to walk through every second of their life and heal every painful memory.

4. Counseling—sharing with the person ways to retain his inner healing. He must be warned that Satan will try to come back against him. He must know to put on the whole armor of the Lord. (Ephesians 6:10-18).

The Lord is the only one who can set the captive free. He is the only one who can save and heal. We, as prayer counselors, can only be imperfect channels of His perfect love. We can only be the tools to help cut away the binding net of black depression, or fear, or whatever has ensnared them. When Lazarus was raised from the dead, Jesus turned to the others

*(See I John 4:4 KJV)

and said, ". . . Unwrap him and let him go!" (John 11:44) Perhaps the Lord will use each of us to help cut loose the binding net around those He sends to us, those who are bound with fear, guilt, depression, rejection, loneliness, etc., that they might be set free. "So if the Son sets you free, you will indeed be free." (John 8:36)

There may be times when the inner healing is instant. There will be times when the healing is a slow process, and the person will become discouraged. There may be times when the person, at that particular time, cannot accept God's healing and forgiveness. You, as prayer counselor and intercessor, need to be loving and sympathetic. When their faith seems to waver, remind them that faith (like salvation) is a gift, it is not something they can "work" for. (See Romans 4:5, 12:3) Pray that they will be given the amount of faith needed.

Then there may, unfortunately, come a time when, after praying and praying, listening, sharing and encouraging a person over a long period of time, the Lord will say, "You have done your part, I have done my part; but until they are willing to do their part, I cannot manifest Myself through them."

The people you pray with will become an extension of yourself—their pains are yours, their joys are yours, their burdens are yours, and their victories are yours. We want to kneel down before Him in adoration and love and honor when ·we think of those who came with heavy hearts and left singing; who came with broken hearts, but left with all the pieces put back in place by the Power and Spirit of God. When we think of those who came bowed down with guilt and shame and left free from those heavy loads; when we remember the marriages which were saved because they allowed Jesus to heal the hurts and the painful memories . . . we cannot praise and thank Him enough.

As I said before, there is not a thing we can do except lift each person up in prayer and watch as the Lord performs His mighty work in each life. Thank you Lord for allowing us to watch and see and be a part . . .

Please remember—

Each of us can continually be ministering God's inner healing to others. Perhaps, not in a two hour scheduled counseling and prayer session, but to every person we come in contact with.

Marjorie Holmes says it so beautifully in **How Can I Find You God?**

> Generosity, giving, sharing, having mercy, being patient, showing compassion, understanding. And no matter what I say, or how many people I help, if I go about this bitterly or grudgingly, then 'it profiteth me nothing.' If I am truly to know and love God, I must have love for his people in my heart.
>
> This means I will be charitable in my spirit as well as my acts. I will refrain from judgements. ('Judge not, that ye be not judged . . .' Who knows what agony lies behind the locked doors of another person's life?) I will not stone a brother or sister with words. ('Inasmuch as ye have done it unto one of the least of these my brethren, ye have done it unto me.')
>
> I will love my neighbors, and show it whenever I can even though I may not tell them so. I will try to love my God with all my heart and soul and mind—and **tell** him so.

Every day let this be our prayer—"God, make me a channel of Your love whereby I might minister Your love and inner healing to those around me—"

Appendix B

Personal Testimonies

In the final pages of this book, Inner Healing, I am including two personal testimonies of people who were touched by the Lord through inner healing.

The testimonies are completely different. One person lived a life of immorality and sin. The other person was a leader in her church and community. But in both cases there were deep, deep hurts and needs.

Whatever your past, whatever your hurts, whatever pain you have, whatever your problems—the Lord wants to meet you at your point of need.

A NEW MIND
(Testimony written by W.J.Z.)*

On May 4, 1975, while lying in a hospital bed, I repeated a sinner's prayer, accepting Jesus as my Savior.

After being discharged from the hospital I realized that having been a lesbian for nearly ten years, an alcoholic for seven years, and a chain smoker for five years, and since I was still smoking and still had a gnawing desire for alcohol and a lustful desire for continuing friendship with the old gang, there must be something more to salvation and a daily walk with JESUS than what I had at this time.

A week or so later during a church service Jesus set me free from all this bondage. However, I still felt burdened with the memory of my old life. It was as though I had a heavy yoke about my neck that caused my head to hang in shame.

A short time later, God's divine providence brought Betty

*Name has been changed.

and Ed into my life and an appointment was made to see them for prayer for inner healing. Time for the appointment came and I arrived at their door with my head still hanging in shame, despondency, and guilt. I was seated and began to relate the same things that I had related to psychiatrists and psychologists time and again. The psychiatrists were only helpful in telling me I should learn to accept myself just as I was. After sharing numerous problems and perfectly horrible memories with Betty, we prayed: and I found in CHRIST JESUS an inner peace that passes all understanding—a freedom and liberty that the world doesn't understand.

Gradually, since this prayer for inner healing, Jesus has brought my subconscious thoughts into my conscious and has given me, not a renewed mind, but a new mind and a heart of forgiveness.

One of the root problems buried in my subconscious mind was revealed by the Holy Spirit as we prayed. At approximately eight years of age I was molested by a neighbor man. This **was** so harrowing that I hid the memory in the deepest recesses of my subconscious. But Praise Jesus, I now can write about it in complete peace and forgiveness.

Then Jesus walked with me through the years shortly following this incident, during which time I lost my father through death. Jesus continued to walk with me through the following years when my mother was ill, and I didn't have the love, care, understanding and feminine example that I needed. The Holy Spirit revealed to me that I had to ask their forgiveness for harboring resentment and anger toward them for something they had no control over. Then, I asked Jesus to take the resentment and anger, and to fill that void with love and peace. He did just that.

Jesus delivered me from the spirit of timidity, and I have boldness as I have never experienced in my entire life. Boldness is especially present when I am witnessing for our Lord. He has taken away the fear, anxiety, and shame which I harbored for years after running over a small child in another country while in a drunken condition.

There are many other memory healings that have taken place in my life, all too numerous to mention, and I praise the Lord for these healings. I also praise the Lord that I can, with clear conscience, say with the Apostle Paul, FOR HE HAS RESCUED ME OUT OF THE DARKNESS AND GLOOM OF SATAN'S KINGDOM AND BROUGHT ME INTO THE KINGDOM OF HIS DEAR SON WHO BOUGHT MY FREEDOM WITH HIS BLOOD AND FORGAVE ME ALL MY SINS. (See Col. 1:13-14)

(Author's Note: This woman later felt the Lord dealing with her about water baptism by immersion and followed the Lord in this ordinance. She said she came up out of the water feeling completely cleansed and forgiven. Several months have passed and she is confidently and gloriously walking with the Lord.)

FROM DEATH TO LIFE
(Testimony written by A.F.W.)*

"My good days are in the past. My hopes have disappeared. My heart's desires are broken." Beside these words of Job (17:11) I wrote 7/74. These digits in the margin would be deceptively innocuous should anyone else pick up my Living Bible, but it would be an indelible reminder that I felt life was over. The future would be a downhill spiral from a once productive life.

The valley experiences were common to me, and on several occasions life had put me in the Red Sea. In all these experiences there was no way but through. I had determination and the faith that God would help me weather the hurt, pain or frustration. Somehow, someday it would all fit into a purposeful plan.

But suddenly, one Sunday morning I was thrust into the midst of the Job experience. Health failed, family problems developed, the close friendship which had been so supportive through the years faltered and pain was my constant companion. The productive life in church, community and home was halted. Along with my decreasing contributions to others came depression, withdrawal, increasing inner anger and resentment.

Each month as the struggle became more desperate, I knew I was making more decisions toward death than life. Though I loved God, the meaningful relationship with Him was choked
*Name has been changed.

off by all the negative things that assailed me. Now the thought of assuming major responsibilities which had once been exciting challenges, paralyzed me with fear. My good days were in the past and so were any worthwhile contributions.

For almost two years grief was my predominate emotion. Tears and deep depression dominated the hours I was alone. Each day brought decreasing physical strength which made it difficult to hang on to spiritual strength.

Obviously my help had to be spiritual, for two clinics and several doctors had been of little assistance. The ministry of inner healing and Betty Tapscott's name kept coming to my mind. The decision was whether I wanted everything known (and life), or whether I preferred secrets (and death). As I approached her door, my emotional state was one of complete dejection . . . but the moment she opened the door, I felt the love, prayer and preparation that had preceeded this meeting . . . Her soft spoken, kindly manner inspired confidence and trust. There would be no condemnation, only empathy, understanding and faith in God to forgive and heal.

In moments she had an overall knowledge of my problems and an insight into a painful memory which affected all my basic realtionships; a painful memory that began before I was born. My parents, after two years of unhappiness, were planning to dissolve their marriage when they discovered that I had been conceived. The news was greeted with tears from my mother and cursing from my father.

During delivery my mother went into convulsions, there seemed no hope of saving my life. The doctor concentrated all his efforts on my mother. Since no one expected me to live, I was hurriedly laid on a table in a corner while frantic efforts were made to save my mother's life. Later when the crisis was over, a nurse walked over to the corner where I had spent the first hour of life alone and unaided. To her astonishment the child was alive.

Thus I was conceived in unhappiness and born under traumatic conditions which allowed the spirit of death, rejection and loneliness to enter in when I was helpless to resist.

From my earliest years I loved God, but these self-destructive feelings always had to be battled. I had confidence when God wanted me to do things, but not much confidence in myself. I could never escape loneliness; it didn't matter how busy I was or how many people were involved. In a way, I was part of the scene, but in a very real sense, I was still that little child off in the corner while the action was going on. Regardless of my achievements and social activities, what I accomplished, and what I did with others never seemed as important or as much fun as the things my friends did. No amount of knowledge or insight changed this. I kept setting higher standards and taking more responsibilities in an attempt to establish my place in life.

And now, exhaustion—spiritual, physical, and emotional—had brought me to my knees in prayer for inner healing. Betty's prayer was a healing balm as her words began to create vivid pictures relating to past memories. She was reliving these experiences with me, but this time the events were from God's perspective.

Ever so gently, lovingly, she said, "Lord Jesus, these parents didn't want this child to be born but **You** did." In that moment God accomplished what knowledge, psychology, logic, and reason had never done. I was not an unfortunate accident, but a life planned and willed by Jesus Christ. As she continued, "Jesus, **You** wanted this child to be born." The feeling that Jesus Himself wanted me was overwhelmingly beautiful. Her gentle words continued, "Lord Jesus, we see You right now going over to that corner, picking up that little baby and putting it on Your shoulder." The painful memory of being cast aside was being healed with the mental image of Jesus holding that frightened infant on His shoulder. I was deeply moved.

"And now, Jesus we see You patting this little baby on the back and clearing all the mucus from its throat." This child who had been unaided by the doctor or nurse was being ministered to by the Lord of heaven and earth. Could anything be more beautiful? The painful memory caused by human failing was healed because the emphasis now was on God's perfect plan. Since our deepest feelings are conveyed in silence, these words cannot express what happened in those moments . . . .

Other needs were prayed for that afternoon. My depressiveness and rejection feelings had allowed related negative feelings to develop. The Holy Spirit revealed that I had always lived with the feeling that I didn't measure up. This led to lack of confidence and eventually to self-destructive feelings. Since I didn't feel loved by my parents, I developed anger, resentment and bitterness, and in turn, guilt and rejection of others.

Several times Betty commented on the loneliness she sensed as she went through events in my life. She prayed for each negative spirit as it was revealed to her by the Holy Spirit.

At one point in her prayer, there was a pause and the question asked if there was severe depression following the birth of one of our children. It was then that she learned that our first child had died at birth. She prayed the sweetest prayer for this little girl. The Holy Spirit had revealed to her that the child was a little girl for I had only said "our first baby."

The third stage of her prayer was for relationships with others. With each member of the family she had me repeat, "I forgive _____ for any hurts she/he may have caused me and I ask forgiveness for any hurts I may have caused them." When she asked me to forgive my father, my voice broke and I could not say, "I forgive my father." I felt a loving hand on my arm. She prayed that I would be filled with forgiveness, that Jesus would forgive through me. When she finished and again asked me to say, "I forgive my father," I could say it and mean it.

Then she prayed for physical wholeness. One immediate discernible answer to this prayer was the extension of my left leg which was half an inch shorter than the right. As she prayed I felt the leg move downward to match soles with the other foot. I felt cleansed, healed, forgiven and accepted. The oppression was gone and strength was returning to my muscles. The Lord healed the arithritis that I had in every joint of my body. Inner peace, joy and thanksgiving flooded my being.

I had arrived broken in spirit, sick in body and feeling totally rejected. Now I was walking away filled in spirit, whole in body and feeling love for everyone . . . .

The world had never been so beautiful as it was that day on a crowded freeway. All the way home I sang praises to God and I am still praising Him. I thank Him for the ministry of Inner Healing. Prayer and God's answer turned me from death to life.

Appendix C

Scriptures on Inner Healing

All quotations are from the Living Bible unless noted otherwise.

Isaiah 53:5 . . . he was wounded and bruised for our sins. He was chastised that we might have peace; he was lashed—and we were healed!

Romans 12:2 (KJV) And be not conformed to this world: but be ye transformed by the renewing of your mind.

John 14:27 I am leaving you with a gift—peace of mind and heart! And the peace I give isn't fragile like the peace the world gives. So don't be troubled or afraid.

Luke 10:27 . . . you must love the Lord your God with all your heart, and with all your soul, and with all your strength, and with all your mind . . . .

Philippians 4:7 . . . His peace will keep your thoughts and your hearts quiet and at rest as you trust in Christ Jesus.

Colossians 1:13, 14 For he has rescued us out of the darkness and gloom of Satan's kingdom and brought us into the kingdom of his dear Son, who bought our freedom with his blood and forgave us all our sins.

II Corinthians 3:17 (KJV) Now the Lord is Spirit: and where the Spirit of the Lord is, there is liberty.

Matthew 18:18 . . . whatever you bind on earth is bound in heaven, and whatever you free on earth will be freed in heaven.

Hebrews 13:8 Jesus Christ is the same yesterday, today, and forever.

Philippians 3:13 Forgetting the past and looking forward to what lies ahead.

Hebrews 4:12 For whatever God says to us is full of living

power; it is sharper than the sharpest dagger, cutting swift and deep into our innermost thoughts and desires with all their parts, exposing us for what we really are.

Hebrews 4:13 He knows about everyone, everywhere. Everything about us is bare and wide open to the all-seeing eyes of our living God; nothing can be hidden from him to whom we must explain all that we have done.

Romans 14:17 (KJV) For the kingdom of God is not meat or drink; but righteousness, and peace, and joy in the Holy Ghost.

Exodus 20:5 (KJV) . . . for I the Lord thy God am a jealous God, visiting the iniquity of the fathers upon the children unto the third and fourth generation of them that hate me.

John 14:12 (KJV) Verily, verily, I say unto you, He that believeth on me, the works that I do shall he do also; and greater **works** than these shall he do; because I go unto my Father.

Ephesians 3:16 . . . out of his glorious, unlimited resources he will give you the mighty inner strengthening of his Holy Spirit.

Psalms 18:2 (KJV) The Lord is my rock, and my fortress, and my deliverer . . .

I Peter 1:22 Now you can have real love for everyone because your souls have been cleansed from selfishness and hatred when you trusted Christ to save you . . .

Matthew 12:35, 36 (Phillips) . . . A good man gives out good—from the goodness stored in his heart; a bad man gives out evil—from his store of evil.

James 4:7 So give yourselves humbly to God. Resist the devil and he will flee from you.

Hebrews 12:15 . . . Watch out that no bitterness takes root among you, for as it springs up it causes deep trouble, hurting many in their spiritual lives.

Joel 2:32 (KJV) . . . whosoever shall call on the name of the Lord shall be delivered . . .

Luke 10:19 (KJV) Behold, I give unto you power to tread on serpents and scorpions, and over all the power of the enemy: and nothing shall by any means hurt you.

Malachi 4:6 His preaching will bring fathers and children together again, to be of one mind and heart . . .

Psalms 51:10 Create in me a new, clean heart, O God, filled with clean thoughts and right desires.

Psalms 147:3 He heals the brokenhearted, binding up their wounds.

Galatians 5:22, 23 But when the Holy Spirit controls our lives he will produce this kind of fruit in us: love, joy, peace, patience, kindness, goodness, faithfulness, gentleness and self-control . . .

Ephesians 2:14 For Christ himself is our way of peace . . .

Isaiah 26:3 He will keep in perfect peace all those who trust in him, whose thoughts turn often to the Lord!

Luke 4:18, 19 "The Spirit of the Lord is upon me . . . he has sent me to heal the brokenhearted and to announce that captives shall be released and the blind shall see, that the downtrodden shall be freed from their oppressors, and that God is ready to give blessings to all who come to him."

1 Thessalonians 5:23 May the God of **peace** himself make you entirely pure and devoted to God; and may your **spirit** and **soul** and **body** be kept strong and blameless until that day when our Lord Jesus Christ comes back again.

Acknowledgments

The *Living Bible,* Tyndale House Publishers Inc., © 1975. Wheaton, Illinois. Used by Permission.

Excerpts from *Something More* by Catherine Marshall Le Sourd © 1974. McGraw-Hill Book Company. Used by permission.

Excerpts from *The Art of Understanding Yourself* by Cecil Osborne. © 1967. Zondervan Publishing House. Used by permission.

Excerpt from *Pigs in the Parlor* by Frank and Ida Mae Hammond. © 1973. Impact Books, Inc. Used by permission.

Phillips, J. B. *The New Testament in Modern English, Revised Edition* © J. B. Phillips 1958, 1960, 1972. The MacMillan Company. Used by permission.

KJV—King James Version.

Excerpts from *How Can I Find You God* by Marjorie Holmes. © 1975 by Marjorie Holmes Mighell. Reprinted by permission Doubleday and Co., Inc.